BUSINESS THE

BILL
GATES
WAY

THE UNAUTHORIZED GUIDE TO DOING BUSINESS THE

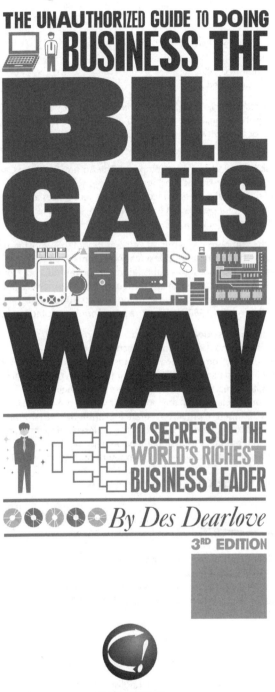

BILL GATES WAY

10 SECRETS OF THE WORLD'S RICHEST BUSINESS LEADER

By Des Dearlove

3RD EDITION

CAPSTONE

Third edition published 2010
© 2010 Des Dearlove
First edition published 1998
Second edition published 2002

Registered office
Capstone Publishing Ltd. (A Wiley Company), The Atrium, Southern Gate, Chichester, West Sussex, PO19 8SQ, United Kingdom
For details of our global editorial offices, for customer services and for information about how to apply for permission to reuse the copyright material in this book please see our website at www.wiley.com.

Library of Congress Cataloging-in-Publication Data

Dearlove, Des.
 The unauthorized guide to doing business the Bill Gates way : 10 secrets of the world?s richest business leader / Des Dearlove. -- 3rd ed.
    p. cm.
 Includes bibliographical references and index.
 ISBN 978-1-907312-46-5 (pbk.)
 1. Gates, Bill, 1955- 2. Microsoft Corporation--Management. 3. Entrepreneurship--United States. 4. Success in business--United States. I. Title.
 HD9696.2.U62G374 2010
 658--dc22
                              2009054398

A catalogue record for this book is available from the British Library.

Set in Myriad Pro by Sparks (www.sparkspublishing.com)
Printed in Great Britain by TJ International Ltd, Padstow, Cornwall

CONTENTS

ACKNOWLEDGEMENTS

I'd like to think this is a fair analysis of why Bill Gates has been so successful over so many years. In the end, though, whether you see him as the Antichrist of the IT revolution or its Messiah or, to a new generation, Bill Gates the philanthropist, battling against global hunger and disease, it is impossible to escape the conclusion that he is a remarkable individual.

For three decades he dominated the computer industry. More than just a computer whiz-kid, Gates also provided a model for business leadership in the 21st century. For this, he deserves acknowledgement. Now he is setting out to create a new chapter in his life, harnessing his considerable intellect, talent, and financial resources to pursue new goals to help society – rather than retire with his billions. For this he deserves our admiration.

Others also merit a special mention. I would particularly like to thank Randall E. Stross, James Wallace and Jim Erickson for their outstanding books on Microsoft, which were an inspiration. I would also like to thank Mark Allin, Richard Burton and Catherine Meyrick at Capstone Publishing who enabled me to write this book the first time round – and Jenny Ng and the new team at Capstone who made it possible this time.

Finally, I would like to say a very special thank you to Steve Coomber for his superb work on the original book and again on this new edition. Steve, it couldn't have been written without you!

Des Dearlove, Forest Row, 2010

BILL GATES, A NEW CHAPTER

When *Business The Bill Gates Way* was published in 2002, it was at a time of great uncertainty for both Gates and Microsoft, the company that he founded all those years ago in 1975.

Perhaps the biggest issue at the time for Gates was the protracted antitrust battle fought in the US. Much of his time and energy was channelled into fighting the antitrust suit brought against Microsoft, which alleged that the company used a dominant market position to restrict competition. A central allegation related to Microsoft's 'bundling' of its web browser Internet Explorer with its Windows operating system. Manufacturers were therefore obliged to pre-install the Microsoft browser on their machines. There were also accusations relating to Windows' compatibility with competing products like Netscape's Navigator web browser.

When the verdict came in April 2000, Judge Jackson, the presiding judge, ruled that the software giant had broken US competition laws. As a result on 7 June, 2000 he ordered Microsoft to be broken up into two separate companies. Naturally, Gates was both dismayed and furious at the decision. Not one to back down, he immediately appealed against the decision. Eventually, the Department of Justice decided against a break up, and various antitrust penalties were imposed, such as a requirement for Microsoft to share some of its intellectual property, such as source code, with third parties.

As soon as one battle finished, though, another began as the European Union launched an abuse of dominant position case against Microsoft relating to the bundling of its Windows Media Player. When Gates was interviewed by the *Seattle Post-Intelligencer* newspaper in June 2008 he was asked about the antitrust case in the US. Gates replied, in humour: 'Well, I don't know why you highlight the US, I mean, why not highlight Japan, Korea, Europe. Come on! We're a global company.'

Microsoft Corporation was shifting direction too. The technology and computing world was changing, and fast. A smallish company, founded just four years earlier, was one cloud on the horizon. Originally just a very smart search engine, Google was shaping up to play an important role in an Internet dominated business age. Apple, under a returning Steve Jobs had regained some of its crunch, launching a small smartly designed gadget – the iPod – in 2001. The founding of MySpace was just around the corner in 2003, heralding the beginning of social networking and Web 2.0.

A sign of the changing times was Microsoft's foray into the computer gaming hardware business. With the Xbox game console Microsoft went head-to-head with Sony and Nintendo, not just for the video games market but also because once video games consoles began offering access to the Internet without a Microsoft operating system or browser, they threatened to cut Microsoft off from a large segment of the population. In the event the outcome was a score draw; Microsoft failed to dominate the video console market, but did enough to spoil Sony's ambitions of dominance.

THE LIFE AND TIMES OF BILL GATES

THE GATES PHENOMENON

Love him or loathe him, Bill Gates is a business phenomenon: the greatest of the techno-savant tycoons. His grip on the PC software market made him the richest man on the planet. It has become a popular pastime in bars and restaurants to astound friends and acquaintances with calculations of his wealth and spending power. It is tempting to believe that there has never been another business leader so loaded. In fact, there have been other mega-rich businessmen, John D. Rockefeller and Andrew Carnegie to name just two. But Gates' wealth is only part of his fascination.

His meteoric rise to fame and fortune confirmed the creation of a new business world order: one that is dominated by a different class of entrepreneur and business leader. We may like to label them nerds, but they know things that most of us don't. They understand the potential of the new technology in a way that the traditional generalist manager and bean counting accountant can't hope to. They are smart; very, very smart about stuff we don't really understand, and it makes the rest of us uncomfortable.

When it comes to the future, they 'get it', and we don't. Technically literate and intellectually elitist, Gates was and is a sign of the leaders to come. To some in Microsoft he was a mystical, almost religious figure (indeed he remains so to many, despite his departure from the business), while to others in the industry he was the Antichrist. Both views are outrageous, but underline just how powerful his influence has been. (With all the hullabaloo about alleged abuses of monopoly power, it is easy to forget that back in the 1970s, IBM, too, was the target of antitrust investigations. Yet, memory fades. Some people have come to regard Big Blue as almost saintly compared to Microsoft. Such is the nature of power – we fear most what we understand least.)

But despite his impact on the business world you won't find many clues to the Gates management technique or leadership style in business schools. In fact, the management professors and gurus are strangely silent on what makes the Microsoft chairman and philanthropist so successful. Perhaps they feel slighted. Gates, after all, dropped out of Harvard where he was majoring in law. The academics prefer more conventional business leaders – the traditional company men.

Where, then, should we turn for an insight into what makes this remarkable man tick? Where better than Microsoft's early foray into the online encyclopedia market with Encarta. 'Much of Gates' success rests on his ability to translate technical visions into market strategy, and to blend creativity with technical acumen', it said under the entry for Gates, William, Henry, III. Not bad for a one-line explanation of Gates' remarkable talents.

In the end, though, what sets Bill Gates apart from any other business leader in history is probably the influence that he wielded over our lives. Whereas the power of earlier tycoons was usually concentrated in one sector or industry, through the power of software, Microsoft extends its tentacles into every sphere of our lives.

Media barons like Rupert Murdoch make us uneasy because they have the power to control what appears in our newspapers and on our television screens. But the influence of the people who write software is incalculable. No wonder we feel uncomfortable with Gates' domination of the software market. No wonder he was vilified and attacked.

But beneath the hype and counter-hype, what sort of man is Bill Gates really? Is he some brainy but basically benign computer whiz-kid, who was in the right place at the right time? Or is there something more to the man who could have retired comfortably in his 20s but preferred to carry on working 16-hour days? Stories abound about Gates the genius mathematician and computer programmer, and about the other Gates, the ruthless businessman who went all out to crush the competition. Only by separating the fact from the fiction can we begin to reveal the real Gates. What emerges from this analysis is a far more complicated picture.

This is not simply a story of technical brilliance and enormous wealth. It is one of remarkable business vision and an obsessive desire to win. It is also about a radically different leadership style to anything the business world has seen before. What Bill Gates offers business leaders of the future is a new template, one that brings together characteristics and skills that are much more suited to the challenges of the twenty-first century. With all his faults, Bill Gates has much to teach the next generation of entrepreneurs and executives.

BILL'S BIG IDEA: A COMPUTER ON EVERY DESK AND IN EVERY HOME

Since the early days of Microsoft, Gates pursued his vision of 'a computer on every desk and in every home'. (Interestingly, the original slogan was 'a computer on every desk in every home, running Microsoft software', but the last part was often left off, because it seemed too self-serving.)

Looking back now, the spread of personal computers from the office into the home seems almost inevitable. Hindsight is a wonderful thing. Foresight, however, is much more lucrative, as Gates has shown. It is important to remember, too, that the ubiquitous screens and keyboards that we all take for granted today were the stuff of science fiction just a couple of decades ago. Back in the 1960s when futurists in America tried to predict the trends that were likely to shape society in the rest of the century they completely missed the rise of the PC. It is no coincidence either that the young Gates devoured science fiction books.

This is not simply a story of technical brilliance and enormous wealth. It is one of remarkable business vision and an obsessive desire to win

It is not true that Bill Gates alone was responsible for putting the PC in homes and offices all over the world, any more than Henry Ford was responsible for the rise of the automobile. What the two have in common, however, was the vision to see what was possible, and to play a pivotal role in making that vision a reality.

Gates set about achieving his vision by transforming Microsoft into a major player in the computer industry and using its dominant position to create a platform for the huge growth in applications. What Gates realized very early on was that, in order for his vision to succeed, it was essential that an industry standard be created. He knew, too, that whoever got there first would have a major opportunity to stamp their authority on the computing industry.

Several years before IBM approached Gates to find an operating system for its new PC, Gates was lamenting the lack of a common platform, and predicting that without one the potential of PCs would not be realized. Articles he penned at that time suggest that he had no more idea of the role destiny had in mind for him than anyone else. The fact is, however, that when the opportunity presented itself, Gates saw it for what it was and grabbed it with both hands. He's been doing much the same ever since.

In the early 1980s, Gates masterminded Microsoft's movement from a developer of programming languages to a diversified software company, producing everything from operating systems such as Windows to applications like Word and Excel, as well as programming tools. In the process he transformed the computer industry.

Those who like to criticize him, and accuse him of monopolistic tendencies, might pause once in a while to reflect on where the PC revolution would be right now without the timely, if self-interested, intervention of Bill Gates. In the end, it's hard to argue with the claim that Bill Gates played a major role in ushering in a new technological era.

HOW RICH IS BILL GATES?

Gates is the richest man in the world today. In the 2009 Fortune Billionaires list Gates was placed first (again) with an estimated pot of $40 billion. On that showing though Gates still has a way to go before he is the richest tycoon of all time.

Back in 1998, *Forbes* magazine[1] recalculated the fortunes of past and present businessmen by comparing the Gross National Product (GNP) in their lifetimes with the size of their bank balances. On this measure, Texas oil baron John D. Rockefeller amassed a fortune of $190 billion. In the number two slot was Andrew Carnegie, the steel baron, who would be worth $100 billion today. Cornelius Vanderbilt, the railroad and shipping magnate came third on $95 billion, followed by John Jacob Astor, the real estate and property tycoon, on $79 billion.

THE GEEKS SHALL INHERIT THE EARTH

Gates is one of a few founding CEOs from the technical side of the PC industry who survived and thrived on the business side. He is a bona fide computer nerd.

William Henry Gates III was born in Seattle, Washington, on October 28, 1955. His parents nicknamed him 'Trey' from the III in his name and members of the family never called him anything else. Gates possessed a precocious intellect – he read the family's encyclopedia from beginning to end at the age of eight or nine. (His company Microsoft would later create the first CD-ROM encyclopedia in the world, Encarta.) But his real gift was for mathematics, at which he excelled.

Young Bill was already fascinated with computers by the age of 12 and, with his long-time business partner and friend Paul Allen, was involved with various programming projects throughout high school. With Allen he would later set up Microsoft.

A brilliant student, unlike most gifted children Gates seems to have excelled at everything he did. His passion for winning was also apparent from an early age. At Lakeside, the elitist Seattle private school that attracts some of the brightest students on America's West Coast, his love of mathematics became an obsession with computers. Even at Lakeside, Bill Gates stood out.

As James Wallace and Jim Erikson note in their book *Hard Drive*: 'Even in an environment like Lakeside, where smart kids tended to command respect, anyone as smart as Gates got teased by some of the others.'[2]

According to one classmate: 'Gates most associated with the kids in the computer room. He was socially inept and uncomfortable around others. The guy was totally obsessed with his interest in computers … You would see him playing tennis occasionally, but not much else. Initially, I was in awe of Gates and the others in the computer room. I even idolized them to some extent. But I found that they were such turkeys that I didn't want to be around them. They were part of the reason I got out of computer work … They had developed very narrowly socially and they were arrogant, and I just didn't want to be like that.'[3]

By his junior year, Gates was something of a computer guru to the younger Lakeside hackers

Sour grapes, perhaps? But clearly, Gates and his cronies were exceptional even by Lakeside standards. By his junior year, Gates was something of a computer guru to the younger Lakeside hackers. He would often hold court in the computer room for hours, telling stories about infamous computer hackers.

Gates and some of his computer friends formed the Lakeside Programmers Group, which was dedicated to finding money-making opportunities to use their new-found computer programming skills. But already, a pattern was emerging. As Gates observed later: 'I was the mover. I was the guy who said "Let's call the real world and try to sell something to it."' He was 13 years old at the time.

The remarkable technical rapport with Allen, two years his senior, seems to have developed at this time. Allen's role in the Microsoft story, and that of a small coterie of Lakesiders recruited by the company, is often understated. Gates, Allen, Kent Evans and Richard Weiland – two other members of the Lakeside Programmers

Group – would often spend hours hooked up, first to a minicomputer owned by General Electric, and later to one at the Computer Centre Corporation, sometimes not getting home until the early hours.

So consumed was the young Gates that his parents became worried about their son's new hobby. For a time, they put a stop to his activities, fearing that it was affecting his studies. Gates abstained from computers for almost a whole year. Typical of his insatiable hunger for knowledge, he turned his attention to other subjects. In this period, he read a number of biographies – including those of Napoleon and Franklin Roosevelt. He wanted, he said, to understand how the great figures of history thought.

He also read business books, science books and novels. One of his favorites was *Catcher in the Rye*, and he would later recite long extracts of the book to his girlfriends. Holden Caulfield, the main character, became one of his heroes.

For the time being, however, any plans young Bill might have for forming a software company with his high school friend and fellow hacker were put on hold. His parents insisted that he should go to college; they felt it would be good for him to mix with other students.

His high IQ and massive personal drive ensured him a place at Harvard University. He arrived at America's most respected seat of learning in Cambridge, Massachusetts, in the fall of 1973 with no real sense of direction.

Later, he would say that he went to Harvard to learn from people smarter than he was ... and was disappointed.[4] The comment probably says as much about Bill Gates opinion of himself as it does about Harvard.

Listing his academic major as pre-law, Gates might have been expected to follow in the footsteps of his lawyer father. In reality, however, he had little interest in a career in law, and his parents soon realized that their headstrong son would steer his own course. In their wildest dreams, however, neither of them could have imagined just what a meteoric journey it would be.

As it turned out, a degree from Harvard was not on the cards. In 1975, while still at the university, he teamed up with Paul Allen once more to develop a version of BASIC, an early computer language. Fired up with the new world at his fingertips, in 1977 Gates decided to drop out of Harvard to work full-time at a small computer software company he had founded with his friend two years earlier. The company was called Microsoft.

FROM HARVARD DROP-OUT TO COMPUTER ICON

The rise of Microsoft was both rapid and relentless. Gates soon proved that he combined a bone-deep technical understanding with superb commercial instincts. When ill health forced Allen to leave Microsoft in the early 1980s, Gates' position as leader was confirmed. In the second half of the 1980s, Microsoft became the darling of Wall Street. From a share price of $2 in 1986, Microsoft stock soared to $105 by the first half of 1996, making Gates a billionaire and many of his colleagues millionaires.

But the rise in Microsoft's share price also sig-
naled a new business world order. Management guru Tom Peters observed that
the world changed when the market
valuation of Microsoft exceeded that
of General Motors. On September 16,
1998, the market valuation of Microsoft
passed that of the mighty GM, to become
America's biggest company with a market
value of $262 billion.

**Later, he would
say that he went to
Harvard to learn from
people smarter than
he was ... and was
disappointed**

BUSINESS PHILOSOPHY

Microsoft's history under Bill Gates' leadership was one of almost
uninterrupted growth in one of the most competitive industries in
the world. While Gates remained full-time at the company, it grew
from a two-man operation to one that employed more than 60,000
people, and generated in excess of $60 billion a year in sales.

Microsoft has attributed its success to five factors:

- a long term approach;

- results orientation;

- teamwork and individual drive;

- a passion for its products and customers; and

- continuous customer feedback.

Gates made sure the company hired very bright, creative people and retained them through a combination of excitement, constant challenge, and excellent working conditions. The odd stock option helped, too.

A relaxed, collegiate style and dislike of status symbols was balanced by a demanding attitude towards performance and meeting deadlines. When people left, Microsoft's research suggested that it was because the challenges ran out. But perhaps the most telling test of the Microsoft culture was that so many of the original early employees remained for so long, and indeed continue to do so. A lot of people have become millionaires through taking advantage of the company's stock options. They could easily have retired, but in many cases, for many years, they chose not to.

As one Microsoft manager put it: 'What else would they do with their lives? Where else could they have so much fun?'

SECRETS OF SUCCESS

Careful analysis reveals ten secrets that explain the success of Microsoft and its remarkable CEO. The secrets of doing business the Bill Gates way are:

1 **Be in the right place at the right time.** It's easy to put Microsoft's success down to one extraordinary piece of good luck – securing the contract to supply IBM with the operating system for its first PC. But there is more to this luck than meets the eye. Gates recognized the significance of the IBM deal. He knew that it could change the history of personal computing, and worked tirelessly for more than six months to maximize his chance of 'being lucky'.

2 **Fall in love with the technology.** One of the most important aspects of Microsoft's success was Gates' technological knowledge. He retained control over key decisions in this area. On many occasions he recognized the future direction of technology more clearly than his rivals. He was also prepared to lead the way.

3 **Take no prisoners.** Gates is a fierce competitor. In everything he does, he is driven to win. As a deal maker that made him an extremely tough negotiator. He made no bones about crushing competitors.

4 **Hire very smart people.** 'High IQ people' is a Microsoft term for the very brightest people. From the start, Gates always insisted that the company required the very best minds. He did not suffer technological fools gladly. In some quarters this was seen as elitist and provoked

criticism. But it had a number of positive effects. It enabled the company to recruit many brilliant students straight from college who were attracted by the prospect of working with the very best in their fields.

5   **Learn to survive.** In Microsoft, Bill Gates created a voracious learning machine. It was, he believed, the only way to avoid making the same mistake twice. His competitors weren't so careful.

6   **Don't expect any thanks.** If there is one lesson Bill Gates has learned the hard way it is that fame and infamy are never far apart. You can't expect to become the richest man in the world without making some enemies.

7   **Assume the visionary position.** Bill Gates cast the mold for a new type of business leader. Over the years, he repeatedly demonstrated that he was the closest thing the computer industry had to a seer. His in-depth understanding of technology and unique way of synthesizing data gave him a special ability to spot future trends and steer Microsoft's strategy. It also inspired awe among Microsoft fans while intimidating competitors.

8   **Cover all the bases.** A key element of Microsoft's success is its ability to manage a large number of projects simultaneously. Gates himself is the original multi-tasking man, and is said to be able to hold several different technical conversations at the same time. This remarkable trait was reflected in Microsoft's approach. It meant that the company constantly explored new markets and new software applications; protecting it from missing 'the next big thing'.

9   **Build a byte-sized business.** Relative to its stock market valuation, Microsoft remained a comparatively small company. Internally, the company was constantly split-

ting into smaller units to maintain the optimal entrepreneurial team environment. At times, change was so rapid that Microsoft seemed to be creating new divisions on an almost weekly basis. Gates relied on maintaining a simple structure partly so that he could keep his grip on the company. Whenever he felt that lines of communication were becoming stretched or fuzzy, he had no hesitation in simplifying the structure.

10 **Never, ever take your eye off the ball.** Gates was at the top of his profession for more than three decades. In that time he became the richest man in the world. Yet despite his enormous wealth and achievements, Gates showed no signs of slowing down, while at Microsoft, or now at the Bill & Melinda Gates Foundation. He said when he was at Microsoft full-time, that he was driven by a 'latent fear' that he might miss the next big thing. He had no intention of repeating the mistakes of other once dominant computer companies such as IBM.

And finally: **Know when it's time to move on.** Great CEOs know when it is time to move on to new challenges. The way Gates managed his exit from Microsoft should be a lesson to all leaders. Gates transitioned out of his full-time role at Microsoft gradually and graciously: shifting seamlessly from the challenge of helping to run the software company he co-founded, to bring his immense talents and resources to bear on societal issues such as global health and development, through his philanthropic work at the Bill & Melinda Gates Foundation.

1

BE IN THE RIGHT PLACE AT THE RIGHT TIME

'The nerds have won.'

– Tom Peters, management writer

The position of power that Microsoft enjoys today is the culmination of a business strategy that Bill Gates and his partner Paul Allen formulated many years ago when both were still in their 20s. The key to that success resides in a combination of factors, including the dazzling technical brilliance of the early Microsoft programmers, the enormous energy and ferocious competitiveness of Gates himself, and his unique vision of how the PC revolution could be brought about and the role that Microsoft could play in it.

It's easy to put Microsoft's success down to one extraordinary piece of good luck – securing the contract to supply IBM with the operating system for its first PC. But there was more than just luck involved. Bill Gates understood the significance of the deal. He knew that an operating system providing a common platform could change the history of personal computing. He worked tirelessly for more than six months to ensure that the opportunity, when it came, would fall to Microsoft. In this way he gave luck a helping hand.

When Gates was preparing to pitch for the IBM contract he is said to have told his mother that she would not see him for six months. During this time he virtually lived at the office devoting himself entirely to winning the IBM business. He sensed how important it was.

The main competitor for the deal was a company called Digital Research Inc, which owned the operating system that ran the Apple II, the most successful desktop computer at that time. At a crucial stage of the negotiations, however, the key contact at Digital Research was away on vacation for a month. Gates, who viewed vacations as a sign of weakness, made sure he capitalized on his competitor's absence. He clinched the deal with IBM – a deal that heralded a new era for business.

NERD POWER

From the cradle of the digital revolution, a new kind of business leader was emerging. The nerds were coming and Bill Gates was leading the charge. Gates is the ultimate expression of 'nerd power'. His own rise to fame and fortune personifies a change in the business constellation. Once unfashionable in corporate America, in the wake of the computer revolution the technical experts – or techies – have risen to prominence.

It's easy to put Microsoft's success down to one extraordinary piece of good luck

For the first time ever, a high level of technical understanding was essential to understand the strategic possibilities that the brave new world of information technology opened up. The traditional generalist executive was out of his depth. Many still couldn't even operate the computer on their desk, let alone programme one.

The blue-suited IBMers who had dominated the computer business for decades were wrong-footed by the switch from mainframes to personal computers. Standing on the threshold of the change was Bill Gates, ready to usher in the new paradigm. Gates and Paul Allen, his high school friend and partner in computer language development, were very different to the IBMers. The new entrepreneurs of Silicon Valley didn't wear suits.

The young Gates, with his bottle-glass spectacles, dandruff and acne, and Allen, with his long hair and shaggy beard, provided Americans with a caricature of the nerds they knew at school. More significantly, for the first time corporate America's discomfort with raw intellect and technical expertise was challenged.

The prevailing myth among the business community of America was that grit, determination, luck and sheer hard graft was enough to get on in business. Brains alone were not seen as the distinguishing factor. In fact, they were sometimes seen as a handicap, especially where they were accompanied by a certain social awkwardness and eccentricity. Corporate America didn't like geeks. The new computer whiz-kids flew in the face of the anti-intellectual tradition. As one commentator observed: 'The vocabulary might change – eggheads in the 1950s, nerds in the 1970s – but the message is the same: brains are a liability not an asset'.

Until the 1970s, American business heroes were people like Lee Iacocca, the CEO of Chrysler – more John Wayne than Peewee Herman. But suddenly with the rise of Microsoft and Apple, the geeks were inheriting the business world. The era of nerd power had begun.

Of course, the pejorative use of the word nerd is an indication of the value society attached to a certain set of characteristics and attitudes – a hangover, in fact, from earlier days when physical prowess and being down-to-earth were regarded as more valuable attributes. What we are now experiencing is a shift in values. This is most obvious in the business world, where we are witnessing the rise and rise of the so-called 'knowledge worker'.

The new computer whiz-kids flew in the face of the anti-intellectual tradition

This represents a significant shift in economic power. It has been likened to the change that took place during the industrial revolution when the application of technology in factories altered employment patterns and wealth distribution beyond all recognition. Many experts claim that the onset of the IT revolution represents an even more significant change. The impact on the corporate world is clear for all to see.

THE DOS BOSS

Bill Gates was in the right place at the right time. At a fateful meeting with IBM in 1980 the future of the computer industry – and arguably the entire business world – took an unexpected turn. Executives from Big Blue signed a contract with a small Seattle-based software firm to develop the operating system for its first PC. They thought they were simply saving time by outsourcing a non-core activity to a small contractor. After all, they were in the computer hardware business, where the real money and power lay. But they were wrong. The world was about to change. Unknowingly they were signing over their market leadership position to Bill Gates' Microsoft.

Much has been made of Bill Gates' manipulation of IBM. But the decision to sign the contract with Microsoft was the culmination of a series of mistakes by Big Blue that reflected its complacency at that time. As a result, it frittered away its dominance of the computer industry. One former IBMer likened the culture at Big Blue during that period to the old Soviet bureaucracy, where the way to get ahead was to impress your immediate boss rather than serve the real interests of the people. So it was that a bloated and complacent IBM collided with a hyperactive and hungry Microsoft. The effect was like introducing a fat and sleepy buffalo to a piranha.

Gates was lucky. But had the same opportunity fallen to one of his Silicon Valley peers, the outcome might have been very different.

In Bill Gates, IBM had picked the one man who would not fumble the ball. On such moments does history turn.

Presented with the chance of a lifetime, Bill Gates would make the most of it. What IBM couldn't see, Gates saw very clearly. The world of computing was on the brink of a major change – what the management theorists like to call a paradigm shift. Gates understood in a way that the old IBM guard could not, that software and not hardware was the key to the future. He knew, too, that the muscle of IBM, the market leader, would be required to establish a common standard, or platform, for software applications. That platform would be based on an existing operating system that Gates bought from another company, called QDOS – renamed MS-DOS by Microsoft. But even Gates could not have imagined just how lucrative the deal would be for Microsoft.

HOW IBM FUMBLED THE PC MARKET

IBM was late off the mark with the PC. The company which dominated the main frame computer business failed to recognize the importance – and the threat presented – by the rise of the personal computer. By the time Big Blue decided to enter the PC market in 1980, Apple, which had pioneered the desktop computer, had become a $100 million business.

Frank Cary, IBM chairman at the time, ordered his people to produce an IBM-badged PC by August 1981. Already in catch-up mode, the IBMers put in charge of the project made two fundamental technical errors. Both mistakes came from a single decision to go outside the company for the two critical elements of the new machine – the microprocessor that would be at the heart of the new PC and the operating system. Intel agreed to supply the chips and a small, relatively unknown software company based in Seattle agreed to supply the operating system.

The launch of the IBM PC was initially a commercial success. But the company ended up giving away most of the profits from its PC business to its two partners. Under the initial contract between IBM and Microsoft, Big Blue agreed to fund most of the development costs of MS-DOS, but only Microsoft was allowed to license the system to third parties. This was the killer clause.

As the PC industry exploded, thousands of new competitors entered the market. Virtually all of them ended up using MS-DOS, and paying Bill Gates for the privilege. But IBM's mistakes didn't end there. When it recognized its initial error, IBM failed to renegotiate the licensing contract or to break with Microsoft. Even more mystifying, senior managers at IBM killed an internally developed operating system that could have broken Gates' stranglehold on the PC market.

More than a decade later, IBM was still manufacturing more PCs than any other company, but its personal systems division was losing money. The only companies making large profits in the highly competitive PC business were the suppliers of the microchips and operating systems. To this day, Intel remains the dominant player in the former and Microsoft in the latter.

STAYING LUCKY

Bill Gates was too bright not to realize that if he played his cards right, his operating system MS-DOS could become the industry standard. At that time, the operating system itself was just one of several on the market.

Many inside the computer industry felt that from a purely technical perspective MS-DOS had some serious drawbacks. Apple was already established as the provider of choice for desktop computers. Apple's founders had brought new attitude and culture to the computer business. Apple's machines were popular because they were simpler to operate and fun to use. The company had yet to develop the famous icon-based Apple Macintosh operating system, but the signs were already there that the people at Apple were ahead of the game.

Gates understood in a way that the old IBM guard could not, that software and not hardware was the key to the future

But Gates had an important ally. He had the muscle of IBM behind his operating system. Big Blue had dominated the mainframe business for years and, somewhat belatedly, was preparing to enter the PC market. The credibility of the IBM name would be crucial in the battle ahead. Gates judged rightly that the best opportunity of establishing an industry standard other than one based around the Apple system lay with the arrival in the PC market of the world's most trusted computer manufacturer. For many years, IBM's proud boast was that 'no one ever got fired for buying an IBM.' At that time, it had a reputation for dependability unmatched in the computer world. The IBM PC was bound to take a big slice of the market for desktop computers.

The fact that IBM-badged machines were about to flood the market also meant that the operating system they used would be catapulted into first or second place. Every single PC shipped by IBM would have MS-DOS installed. For Microsoft it was the perfect Trojan Horse. Every IBM-badged PC that landed on a desk gave a free ride to the Microsoft operating system that lay hidden inside. This was Bill Gates' amazing piece of luck. But what happened next goes a long way to explaining why Bill Gates and not Steve Jobs, or some other Silicon Valley entrepreneur, is now the richest man in the world.

By the late 1970s, Microsoft was already licensing its software to a variety of customers. In 1977, Gates supplied software for Tandy, but it also licensed BASIC 6502 to Apple for the Apple II Computer. Microsoft went on to work with many of the other leading computer companies. This suited Bill Gates' purposes perfectly. Microsoft was already beginning to set the industry standard with its software. It was this strategy that he continued with MS-DOS, persuading as many PC makers as possible to license the system and distribute it in their computers.

Microsoft was already beginning to set the industry standard with its software

Apple, on the other hand, took the view that the only way to ensure the quality of its products was to try to retain control of everything. Later this included its proprietary Macintosh operating system.

Apple didn't want anyone else to 'clone' its computer. For years, the company resolutely refused to license its Apple Mac operating system to other manufacturers. This meant that anyone who wanted the user-friendly Apple operating system had to buy an Apple computer. It was a strategy that seemed to make sense – but only by the old rules of the game. The problem for Apple was that in terms of business model and strategic vision, it was only one generation on from the hardware dinosaur IBM.

Apple was in both the hardware and software businesses. Even though its managers recognized the growing value customers attached to the intangible software over the physical hardware, they were unable to divorce the two strategically.

Apple reasoned that they had a killer combination; they reckoned that in the Apple Mac they had the best operating system and the best machine on the market, it was just a matter of time before they dominated the desktop industry. The mistake lay in believing that the best technology will win in the end. They were wrong. By the time they realized their mistake Gates and Microsoft had seized 80 percent of the market. (Had Apple's executives taken a look at the development of the VCR some years earlier, they would have realized that they were not the first to make this mistake. Despite an apparent technological advantage Sony's Betamax video system was eventually eclipsed by the technically inferior VHS system.)

Gates' business savvy won the day. MS-DOS was established as the industry standard. The question was whether Gates could go the distance. By the mid-1980s, Gates' reputation as an outstanding programmer was widely accepted. Few doubted that he was one of the most talented techies to emerge from the maelstrom of the Silicon Valley revolution. His competitive spirit and personal drive to succeed were legendary. What critics questioned were his managerial credentials. They asked whether he had the necessary skills and charisma to lead a company that was fast becoming a major player in corporate America.

As early as 1984, *Fortune* magazine chided him for failing to develop the management depth to turn the temporary victories he had won into long term dominance.[1] What the business press had still to learn was that Gates was much more than just a techie or a computer nerd on a lucky streak. There was a lot more to Bill Gates than met the eye. His ascendancy to the corporate throne marked an important shift in the balance of power in the business world.

MOORE'S LAW

In 1965, in what came to be known as Moore's Law, Gordon Moore, a founder of Fairchild Semiconductor and later of Intel, quantified the rate at which microchips would increase in power. Based on his calculation of the rate at which the technology was advancing, Moore predicted that over the next ten years the number of components that could be fitted on a microchip would continue to double every twelve months.

The concept of setting standards remains at the heart of the Microsoft business strategy

What this meant, in effect, was that the capability of the chips would double every year without adding significantly to the cost. The prediction proved amazingly accurate. But in the early 1970s few people understood what that would mean for the future of the industry. A couple of computer fanatics from Seattle thought they had a clue.

Moore's law inspired Bill Gates and Microsoft co-founder Paul Allen to set up Microsoft. Gates credits Allen with showing him Moore's Law and pointing out the business potential in exponentially improving semiconductor technology. Exponential phenomena are rare, recalls Gates, asking Allen sceptically. 'Are you serious?'

Allen was deadly serious. What he and Gates understood that the suits at IBM and DEC didn't were the implications of this. The two reasoned that if Moore was right then processing power would make micro computers viable in a very short space of time. 'It's going to happen', they said, and they set about preparing to write software for the machines that would follow.

SETTING THE STANDARD

The decision to outsource the operating system to Microsoft was a mistake that cost IBM dearly. Similarly, Apple's decision not to license its operating system was one that subsequently prevented it from taking a larger market share and almost bankrupted the company. These were mistakes that Bill Gates had no intention of repeating.

Those two fateful decisions helped shape the Microsoft culture. There is an awareness that the company that establishes the industry standard will almost always dominate the market. It is a point hammered home to those who work at Microsoft.

'We set the standard', was an unofficial Microsoft slogan even before it signed the deal with IBM. It underlines the clarity of Gates' thinking from the very beginning. It explains his obsession with bringing new products to market first. Where someone got the jump on Gates, it also explains the ferocity with which Microsoft marketed its own version when it came out. In some cases, too, Gates simply bought a software company lock, stock and barrel if he believed it had established a significant technological lead on his own company with an important application. In doing so, he ensured that Microsoft dominated that market from the outset. At the same time, he acquired the technological know-how by bringing the brains behind it into the Microsoft fold.

The concept of setting standards remains at the heart of the Microsoft business strategy, a timely reminder to anyone at Microsoft who might forget the importance of the IBM lesson. Now, of course Gates is setting new standards, but this time in his philanthropic endeavours.

UBIQUISOFT

Love him or loathe him, there is no denying Bill Gates' achievements with Microsoft. The fact is that Microsoft software still dominates the global computer industry. The Windows operating system has over 90 percent market share, meaning that nearly all desktop computers run one or other version of Microsoft's Windows software. Moreover, the vast majority of new PCs are shipped with Microsoft software installed. This gives Microsoft an enormous head start over its rivals.

In the years before Gates stepped down from the day-to-day running of the business, he showed that he was very adept at leveraging Microsoft's dominant position to capture new and emerging application markets. Some say that he used what amounted to a stranglehold on the PC software market to foist Microsoft products onto customers. On the other hand, Gates simply did what any smart businessman should do; press home an advantage.

There was a lot more to Bill Gates than met the eye. His ascendancy to the corporate throne marked an important shift in the balance of power in the business world

It is tempting to look back at the history of personal computing and regard Microsoft's dominant market position as a given. To do so, though, is to view the PC revolution through a narrow lens; to think that the market for PCs would have automatically taken off regardless of the actions of key players such as Bill Gates would be assuming too much. An alternative interpretation is to look at Microsoft's domination as the result of the mistakes of others – principally IBM and Apple. But this, too, is seriously to underestimate the role of Gates and his colleagues at Microsoft.

BE IN THE RIGHT PLACE AT THE RIGHT TIME

In the era of the knowledge worker, technical know-how and creativity are the new corporate assets. Combine these with business acumen and a highly competitive nature and you have a rare bird indeed. Throughout his tenure at the head of the world's most famous software company, Gates exemplified that rare bird. But it was also a remarkable piece of good fortune that carried him to an altitude where his special talents allowed him to soar. The first lessons from the Bill Gates school of business leadership are:

- **Nerd power: let the technology shape your strategy.** Gates was one of the few business leaders who really understood the technology. This enabled him to make strategic decisions based on his own vision of where the technology was heading.
- **Be in the right place at the right time.** Microsoft had a huge dollop of luck in 1980 when IBM, then the market leader in the computer industry, signed a contract with Bill Gates to develop the operating system for its first PC.
- **Stay lucky – don't fumble the ball.** Being lucky only gets you so far; it's what you do with that luck that really counts. There are a great many millionaires in Silicon Valley who might have been billionaires if they had exploited their good fortune as Gates has. When the opportunity of a lifetime dropped into his arms, Gates grabbed it with both hands. He's been scoring touchdowns ever since.
- **He who sets the standard, wins.** What Gates understood that others did not was that in the computer business,

market share is self-perpetuating. Once a company estab-lishes an industry standard it becomes much harder for a newcomer to usurp their position. 'We set the standard' was the unofficial Microsoft motto even in its early days, long before it signed the fateful contract with IBM.

- **Leverage your bits off.** Gates successfully leveraged Microsoft's dominant market position to establish its own versions of new applications. True, Microsoft may have overdone things a little, at least in the eyes of some author-ities. The principle remains though, if you have power, use it to your advantage – within the law, of course.

2

FALL IN LOVE WITH THE TECHNOLOGY

'I actually understand how to write software; there's a whole new world of standards to be developed; my people are smarter about this stuff and nobody else is doing it.'

– Bill Gates

Bill Gates has enjoyed a lifelong love affair with the personal computer. From the very beginning, Gates and his partner Paul Allen could see that the PC would change everything. The two would talk late into the night about what the post-PC world would be like. They never truly doubted that the revolution would come. 'It's going to happen' was an article of faith for the fledgling Microsoft, and they were going to write software for it when it did. What neither could have imagined then was the part they would play or the extraordinary turn of events that catapulted their company onto the world stage. But even then they knew what IBM and other mainframe computer companies such as Digital Equipment Corporation (DEC) didn't – that those companies were in deep, deep trouble.

'I remember from the very beginning, we wondered, "what would it mean for DEC once microcomputers were powerful and cheap enough? What would it mean for IBM?" To us it seemed they were screwed. We thought maybe they'd even be screwed tomorrow. We were saying "God, how come these guys aren't stunned? How come they're not just amazed and scared?"'[1]

Gates' technological knowledge was one of the most important factors in Microsoft's long-term success. For much of his tenure, he retained control over key decisions in that area. On many occasions he was able to see the future direction of technology more clearly than his rivals.

CODE WARRIORS

Gates is one of the few founding CEOs from the technical side of the PC industry who survived and thrived on the business side. His love affair with the technology gave his leadership a distinctive edge. For all his wealth and commercial experience, deep down Gates remained what he was at the start – a techie.

Gates regarded 'writing code' – as computer programming is known – as a higher calling. Employees at Microsoft were divided into two classes: product development groups – which include the top programmers; and everyone else.

Gates himself claims to be able to recall 'huge slabs' of code many years after he has last tinkered with it

The product groups received the lion's share of the stock options; their programmers' private offices at the Microsoft campus at Redmond were defended most vigorously whenever there was a shortage of office space. (In 1995, the squeeze became so intense that smaller product groups were moved into an annex about a mile away from the main campus.)

Former colleagues at Microsoft agree that Gates' technical knowledge gave him an edge. 'He has the ability to ask the right question. He'll know some intricate detail about a program and you wonder: "How does he know that?"' says Brad Silverberg, who was part of the Windows development team.

Gates himself claimed to be able to recall 'huge slabs' of code many years after he had last tinkered with it. In the old days, he would personally review every line of code. As both Microsoft and the CEO's role grew, that was no longer possible. However, Gates retained a keen interest in all new Microsoft products, as was clear when he assumed the title of Chief Software Architect in 2000, even after relinquishing the CEO spot.

'I'm certainly able to use all the products we have', he said, 'but I can't possibly review all the code. My role is more to do with the strategy and the direction people are moving in and how well they work together. There's a lot of invention going on and I have to pick which things are important and express them to the user. It's all very critical.'

Business, on the other hand, requires no special expertise in his view. 'If you're any good at math at all, you understand business – it's not its own deep, deep subject', he observed in 1992. It required just ten percent of his own 'mental cycle', he said.

START YOUNG

Gates preference for recruiting the brightest graduates straight out of college is well known. At first, the company simply hired clever people Gates and his partner Paul Allen knew from school. These they called 'smart friends'. But by the time Microsoft moved from Albuquerque to Seattle, at the end of 1978, it had run out of smart friends and had to start recruiting 'smart strangers'.

Over the years, the company developed its own special recruitment techniques and preferences. From the very beginning, Gates recognized that his approach to developing software could best be nurtured among 'very young people, fairly inexperienced'.

So by 1994 when the average age of Microsoft employees had risen to 31, Gates confessed that he would like to see the percentage of employees hired direct from college return to the 80 percent it had been in the early years. 'Young people are more willing to learn, and come up with new ideas', he said.[2]

Gates' own love affair with computers began when he was at school. At that time, few schools could afford to provide their students with access to a computer, but Lakeside, the school he attended, was an exception. Gates made his first deal in the computer business at the tender age of 13 when he agreed to look for software bugs in return for free computer time.

'I was lucky enough when I was quite young to have an exposure to computers, which were very expensive and kind of limited in what they could do, but still they were fascinating', he observed.

The prevailing logic at that time was that computers belonged in offices and would remain there. But to Gates and his friends, the potential was much greater

For the young Gates, the discovery of computers opened up a whole new world. What he and his teenage friends could see that adults already working in the computer industry could not was the enormous potential of the computer to change people's lives.

The prevailing logic at that time was that computers belonged in offices and would remain there. But to Gates and his friends, the potential was much greater.

'Some friends of mine and I talked about that a lot and decided that, because of the miracle of chip technology, they would change into something that everybody could use. We didn't see any limit to the computer's potential, and we really thought writing software was a neat thing. So we hired our friends who wrote software to see what kind of a tool this could really be – a tool for the Information Age that could magnify your brainpower instead of just your muscle power.'

The other great advantage that Bill Gates and his Microsoft cronies had was that they were involved with the development of personal computing from its earliest days. 'By pursuing that with a pretty incredible focus and by being there at the very beginning of the industry, we were able to build a company that has played a very central role in what's been a pretty big revolution', said Gates in a question and answer session along with fellow billionaire Warren Buffet in 1998. 'Now, fortunately, the revolution is still at the beginning. It was 23 years ago when we started the company. But there's no doubt that if we take the habits we formed and stick with them, the next 23 years should give us a lot more potential and maybe even get us pretty close to our original vision – "a computer on every desk and in every home."'

'We didn't see any limit to the computer's potential ...'

Bill Gates

But while youth fuelled their ambition and sense of the possible, it also created some problems. When they first set up Microsoft, Gates and his partner Paul Allen had trouble getting other parts of the industry to take them seriously. As Gates explained: 'At first you'll run into some skepticism. If you're young, it's hard to go lease premises. You couldn't rent a car when you were under 25, so I was always taking taxis to go see customers. When people would ask me to go have discussions in the bar, well, I couldn't go to the bar.'

Youth also had its advantages, however. For one thing, it meant that Gates' business acumen was often underestimated in the early days. As Jack Sams, one of the IBM executives who signed the contract with the 21-year-old Gates to supply the operating system for the first IBM PC, recalled: 'When he came out, I thought he was the office boy.'

It was a mistake that IBM would regret. Gates was aware of the impression that his youth created, and used it to good advantage.

'That's fun', he observed years later, 'because when people are first skeptical, they say, "Oh, this kid doesn't know anything.' But when you show them you've really got a good product and you know something, they actually tend to go overboard. So, at least in this country, our youth was a huge asset for us once we reached a certain threshold.'

GEEK CHIC

What the socially awkward Gates also achieved at Microsoft was to make software development fashionable for the first time. In part, this was simply the result of the large sums of money that could be earned from developing good products. But it went further. When Gates and his Lakeside friends first started hanging out in the school's computer room, they were regarded as geeks. But then as companies such as Microsoft and rival Apple became better known, public perception started to change.

By the mid-1980s it was 'cool' to be into computers. Throughout America, the brightest college students had a new career in mind. They couldn't wait to finish school to get out to Silicon Valley or the Microsoft campus at Redmond, where things were really happening. Microsoft had its own special hip culture and slant on the business.

By then, Gates and his colleagues at Microsoft had invented their own language, based on slang they used as school yard computer hackers. Examples include:

- Dogfooding – internal use of software products – usually in beta form complete with bugs and glitches – as part of the development process. Hence, 'eating your own dogfood'.

- Selftoast – to contradict yourself.

- Vaporware – a product that never reached the shelves, for one reason or another.

- Facemail – having a conversation in the same room (as opposed to voicemail or email).

- Braindump – passing on technical knowledge.

R&D FOREVER

Coming from the technical side, Bill Gates understood the importance of investing in research. He invested an extraordinarily high percentage of Microsoft's revenues in research and development. So much so that in 1984, *Forbes* magazine, which compiles an annual list of the richest people in the world, observed that Gates would never appear in its annual review of America's richest people, because, it said, he poured so much money into R&D. (As it turned out Gates was ranked #1 in the *Forbes* rich list for 13 straight years, before temporarily relinquishing his title to buddy Warren Buffet for 2008, only to regain his title of world's richest man in 2009.)

Gates acknowledges that the disproportionately high research budget is one of the main reasons for Microsoft's success, but says it is one that other companies could easily imitate. By pouring huge amounts of the company's revenues into R&D, Gates ensured that Microsoft was always prospecting for the next big thing. In its software laboratories Microsoft is developing products for many years down the road.

GM VERSUS MICROSOFT

Management guru Tom Peters points to a day in mid-1992 as the day the world changed.[3] At that moment, the stock market valuation of Microsoft exceeded that of General Motors for the first time. On that day Wall Street put a higher value on Microsoft, which owns virtually no physical assets, than it did on GM, with all its factories, offices and inventory. The idea would have been unthinkable just a few decades ago.

By investing so much of the company's revenues in R&D, Gates constantly added to Microsoft's reservoir of intellectual capital. According to Johan Roos, president of Copenhagen Business School, GM symbolizes the industrial era, whereas Microsoft symbolizes the new era of information.[4]

Gates acknowledges that the disproportionately high research budget is one of the main reasons for Microsoft's success

How can you explain the switch? 'The crux is that it is individuals who are the chief source of competitive advantage, rather than the physical assets the company owns and controls', observed Professor Roos.

'… Intellectual capital as a concept says more about the future earnings capabilities of a company than any of the conventional performance measurements we currently use. If the top fifty programmers suddenly left Microsoft, the share price would probably drop dramatically.'

DON'T REINVENT THE WHEEL

Microsoft's rivals claim that the company is not good at innovation and has a poor track record for creating software from scratch. Mike Zisman, vice president, corporate strategy, IBM, and former CEO of Lotus (a long time Microsoft rival) observed, while still at Lotus: 'I don't worry about Microsoft. It never invented anything.' But the bravado masks the real strength of the software wizards of Redmond: they are very, very good at taking ideas and turning them into usable products. (Lotus was eventually acquired by IBM).

In fact, Gates does not necessarily rate people who are obsessed with original solutions to problems. Most people only have one brilliant idea in their entire lifetimes, he has said. Most solutions already exist somewhere and simply have to be identified. This was his great talent with Microsoft – identifying solutions, acquiring them and developing them into commercially successful products.

Even DOS, the operating system that made Microsoft famous, was not invented by Gates. His partner Paul Allen bought a version of the operating system called QDOS from another computer company, Seattle Computers, for $50,000. Microsoft developed it and supplied it to IBM for its first PC. Gates and Allen made billions of dollars as a result.

The Microsoft that Gates ran was not necessarily the most innovative company in the world, but its ability to take ideas and make them into commercial propositions was second to none. What Bill Gates demonstrated many times over is that innovation and R&D are not necessarily the same thing. In many cases, the emphasis is on researching how customers want to use an application and developing a marketable product that meets their requirements. Pure innovation, Gates believed, was overrated. He preferred to look around for existing solutions which could then be refined, rather than to constantly reinvent the wheel.

Microsoft was also good at shaping the future direction of technology, most noticeably the spread of multimedia. In the early days of CD-ROM, for example, when the technology was struggling to be accepted, Gates funded a series of conferences to promote the CD-ROM concept. These events championed the cause of the new technology and placed Microsoft at the centre of the CD-ROM movement.

This was his great talent with Microsoft – identifying solutions, acquiring them and developing them into commercially successful products

When it still failed to catch on, Gates realized that there was a chicken and egg problem. Hardware manufacturers were not going to include CD-ROM drives on their systems until someone produced some CD-ROM titles users could buy. By the same token, no one wanted to invest in developing CD-ROM titles until the hardware was there to play them. The result was a stalemate that threatened to block the new technology. Gates instructed his developers to create some CD-ROM titles double quick. The result was a series of reference titles that led eventually to the creation of Encarta, the first multimedia encyclopaedia. CD-ROM took off.

It was his love affair with the computer that kept Bill Gates at the forefront of the IT industry, an industry where you can all too easily lose the plot. 'The key point is that you've got to enjoy what you do every day', he said. 'For me, that's working with very smart people and it's working on new problems. Every time we think, "Hey, we've had a little bit of success", we're pretty careful not to dwell on it too much because the bar gets raised. We've always got customer feedback telling us that the machines are too complicated and they're not natural enough. The competition, the technological breakthroughs and the research make the computer industry, and in particular software, the most exciting field there is, and I think I have the best job in that business.'5

FALL IN LOVE WITH THE TECHNOLOGY

The second set of lessons from the Bill Gates school of business is:

- **Understand your business.** In the era of the knowledge worker, when the company was asserting, establishing and cementing its position, it took a techie to run a company like Microsoft. Only someone with a bone deep knowledge of the technology could truly understand what was going on in the industry, identify the trends, and set a winning strategy.
- **Create a business culture that recognizes the importance of technical experts.** Most companies have traditionally valued generalists more highly than specialists. At Microsoft the software developers are regarded as more important than managers.
- **Start young.** Gates' love affair with computers began when he was at school. At that time, few schools could afford to provide their students with access to a computer. But Lakeside, the school he attended, was an exception. Gates made his first deal in the computer business at the tender age of 13 when he agreed to look for software bugs in return for free computer time.

- **Invest more than anyone else.** By pouring huge amounts of the company's revenues into R&D Gates ensured that Microsoft was always prospecting for the next big thing. In its software laboratories Microsoft develops products for many years down the road.
- **Lead technology to shape the future.** Although Microsoft is not a prodigious inventor, it has always been extremely adept at taking good ideas, developing them and making them into commercially successful products. In fact, Gates does not necessarily rate people who are obsessed with original solutions to problems. Most people only have one brilliant idea in their entire lifetimes, he says. He believes that most solutions already exist somewhere and simply have to be identified. This, he has claimed, is his own great talent. Gates has also proved willing to use Microsoft's muscle to champion new technologies such as multimedia which then shape the future.

3

TAKE NO PRISONERS

'Gates is tenacious. That's what's scary …
he always comes back, like Chinese water
torture. His form of entertainment is tearing
people to shreds.'

– Stewart Alsop, editor of *PC Letter*

Bill Gates was a fierce competitor during his tenure at Microsoft's helm, and addicted to winning. This made him an extremely tough adversary. He made no bones about this, talking openly about crushing the competition. He took no prisoners, and marketed the company's products aggressively.

The marketing of Microsoft products, including the frequent upgrades that make earlier versions of software obsolete, ruffled a lot of feathers inside the US Government. These and other concerns, including a series of complaints from rivals in the computer industry, aroused the interest of the Federal antitrust authorities, which investigated Microsoft for alleged anti-competitive practices – as did the European Commission of the European Union – in what seemed an endless round of rulings, counterclaims, fines and settlements.

In 1998, for example, the US Justice Department and 20 US states brought an anti-competition case against Microsoft related to alleged breaches of an earlier ruling concerning the packaging of the Internet Explorer web browser with the Windows OS. In the first instance, the finding went against Microsoft in a ruling, part of which stipulated that Microsoft should be split into two divisions. Microsoft appealed, however, and the Department of Justice, while not overturning the findings of fact, overturned the original remedy agreeing a settlement with Microsoft to share its application programming interfaces knowledge with third-party companies.

Gates vigorously defended the company's marketing strategy, claiming Microsoft had a positive impact on consumer choice. While opinions remain divided over whether the eventual settlement was appropriate, there is no doubt that, as Microsoft CEO, Gates was a formidable competitor and superb marketing strategist. According to *Fortune* magazine, every successful enterprise requires three men: a dreamer, a businessman, and a son-of-a-bitch. 'Bill Gates has all three qualities, making him stand out as the most successful start-from-nothing businessman the world has ever known.'

Indeed it is telling that when Gates talked about the competition he would lump them all together. Yet when competitors talked about Gates, they singled him out.

LEVERAGE YOUR BITS OFF

What Gates was unquestionably good at was leveraging Microsoft's market position to provide access to new and emerging markets. The reality is that, if you own the operating system that runs a large majority of the desktop computers in the world, that gives you a lot of negotiating and marketing muscle. Not only does it generate huge amounts of cash to be reinvested in new product research and development, it also provides unique opportunities for the packaging or bundling of software products.

On a number of occasions Gates used his dominant market position to make life extremely difficult for his competitors. He has never been afraid to go to war with a big competitor, as he showed when Apple decided that the take-up of the Windows graphical interface gave Gates too much power, or later with Apple–IBM, when the two IT giants joined forces to topple him, or with Borland with which Gates fought a database war.

Such was his success in these and other turf wars that the smart money in Silicon Valley rarely if ever bet against Microsoft. Leverage is something Gates did better than anyone else; a pragmatic and logical approach based on maximizing his market position.

IF YOU CAN'T BEAT THEM, BUY THEM

Gates' pragmatism also extended to buying his way into key markets. He was quite prepared to go out and buy the development expertise of other companies and then plug it into the Microsoft machine. Faced with a need to create database products to compete with Borland, for example, Gates went out and spent $170 million buying the software that had already been developed by another company.

The reality is that, if you own the operating system that runs a large majority of the desktop computers in the world, that gives you a lot of negotiating and marketing muscle

In fact, this is a strategy that Gates used many times. In 1982, for example, he bought the basis of DOS from a small company called Seattle Computers, and went on to make it into the industry standard. And it's not just software that he plundered. On occasions, Gates bought companies simply to acquire the expertise of exceptional programmers, who would often have a stake in the smaller firm. In such cases, Gates could offer several million dollars for the company as an inducement for the key individuals to join Microsoft. In this way, he brought deep seams of technical expertise into Microsoft very rapidly.

'We've bought a lot of small companies, and I'd say that's been vital to us', he noted. 'These are companies that on their own probably wouldn't have made it, but when their abilities are combined with ours, both of us were able to create a much better set of products than we could have otherwise.'

SLEEPING WITH THE ENEMY

For all his fighting talk, Bill Gates did not allow grudges to affect his commercial decisions. The ultimate pragmatist, on many occasions Gates has fought a pitched battle with a rival for years, only to turn around and do business with them when it suits him. In almost every case, it is on his terms.

He happily poured money into Apple, for example, to shore up the company that had been attacking his market position for years.

Whereas many business leaders become locked into an aggressive stance, allowing their personal grudges to dictate their decisions, Gates was always rational. Critics claim that he allowed his emotions to get the better of him in some cases – in particular, that his dislike of certain rivals sometimes clouded his judgement. On the contrary, like a spoilt child that throws a tantrum to get its way, Gates may have personalized a battle for a time, but only to focus Microsoft's fire.

In a passionate industry, Gates demonstrated a remarkable ability to keep personalities out of business decisions. Whatever he did– even if it proved ruinous to another company – it was for a purely commercial end. What mattered to Gates was winning; in order to do so he wanted to beat the enemy, but that didn't mean he wouldn't work with them at a later date. That made him a far more dangerous adversary than someone who is hot-headed or acts out of emotion.

Competing with Bill Gates was like playing chess. He always thought many moves ahead and punished his opponents' blunders with cold-blooded predatory indifference. That's why so many people in the industry feared him.

RISK MANAGEMENT

Along with his analytical and detached approach to business, Gates was also a shrewd judge of risk. This is something he learnt along the way. But where others who are risk averse have a tendency to delay decisions, Gates was only too aware that in the computer industry the speed of change is so rapid that not acting often carries the greatest risk of all. Risk has to be balanced against reward.

'If you're going to start a company, it takes so much energy that you'd better overcome your feeling of risk', said Gates back in 1998.

'Also, I don't think that you should necessarily start a company at the beginning of your career. There's a lot to be said for working for a company and learning how they do things first. In our case, Paul Allen and I were afraid somebody else might get there before us. It turned out we probably could've waited another year, in fact, because things were a little slow to start out, but being on the ground floor seemed very important to us.

'I was so excited that I didn't think of it as being all that risky. It's true, I might have gone bankrupt, but I had a set of skills that were highly employable. And my parents were still willing to let me go back to Harvard and finish my education if I wanted to.

'The thing that was scary to me was when I started hiring my friends, and they expected to be paid. And then we had customers that went bankrupt – customers that I counted on to come through. And so I soon came up with this incredibly conservative approach that I wanted to have enough money in the bank to pay a year's worth of payroll, even if we didn't get any payments coming in. I've been almost true to that the whole time.'

RAM BEAU

Gates was relentless, too. He played poker in the computer industry, probably the most frantically competitive industry in the world, for over three decades. A multi-billionaire while still a young man, he could have retired from Microsoft much earlier than he did. Today, with his philanthropic activities at the Bill & Melinda Gates Foundation, coupled with his non-executive chairman position at Microsoft, he seems to cram as much, if not more, into his year than he did as Microsoft CEO.

Many of his industry peers from the days when he started the business out either bowed out, or stepped back, before him. That included his former partner Paul Allen (he left Microsoft as a result of ill-health when he was diagnosed as suffering from Hodgkin's disease). Gates was one of the few to stick around in the war zone, along with IT heavyweights such as Steve Jobs at Apple, Larry Ellison at Oracle, and Scott McNealy at Sun Microsystems.

What mattered to Gates was winning; in order to do so he wanted to beat the enemy, but that didn't mean he wouldn't work with them at a later date

Many dropped out to write books, start new companies or chill out. Not Gates – he wrote his books *The Road Ahead* (1996) and *Business @ the Speed of Thought* (1999) whilst running his business, fending off antitrust allegations and developing a strategic response to prospering as a business in the Internet age. As he observed when asked about his plans to become a key player in Internet technology, 'The fact is that most of our operating systems competitors seem fatigued. Fine, now we have got new competitors. It is always fun to be the underdog.'[1] One thing is for certain, under Gates' watch, the underdog had a fierce bite.

GATES ON COMPETITION LAW

Critics of Gates and Microsoft complained frequently that the company was adept at using its commercial might to squash competition in its market. Whether it was pre-announcing planned products to forestall new rivals, tying other Microsoft products to the pre-installed Windows operating system, snapping up all the potential competitors in a nascent market, or implementing anti-competitive rebating schemes with original equipment manufacturers, the accusations came thick and fast.

Despite the numerous complaints levelled against Microsoft and the court cases and EU Commission rulings, Gates maintained a staunch defence of his company. He robustly denied that Microsoft abused its market position, stoutly defending the company's impact on the PC market. Microsoft, he felt, was the victim of unfair accusations of jealous rivals seeking to shore up their competitive position via the government or other international bodies. Rather than being anticompetitive, argued Gates, Microsoft had created the conditions necessary for the personal computing revolution, bringing society changing gains for consumers, falling prices, and a great number and variety of new products and innovations. And he had a point.

'You have to remember that before personal computers came along, the structure was very different. People were stuck. Once you bought a computer from Digital or IBM or Hewlett-Packard or anyone else, the software that you created only ran on that computer', said Gates.[2]

'The vision of Microsoft was that all of these computers would work the same. The reason for that is that if you want to get a lot

of great software, you have to have a lot of computers out there –
millions and millions of them. So you've got to make them cheap,
and make them so you don't have to test the software on all the
different ones. The goal of the PC industry was to have every
company competing to make the most port-
able one, or the fastest one, or the cheapest
one. That would be great for consumers,
and it would spark a big software market.'

Rather than being anticompetitive, argued Gates, Microsoft had created the conditions necessary for the personal computing revolution

'Part of the PC dynamic is that instead of
asking software developers to duplicate
one another's work, we take anything
that's typical in all those applications and
put those features in Windows. So for things
like connecting to the Internet, instead of
everybody having to do that themselves, we
put that in. That's been the evolution – graphi-
cal user interfaces came in, hard-disk support, networking support,
now Internet support, including the browser.'

TAKE NO PRISONERS

Gates is a fierce competitor. In everything he does, he is driven to win. This makes him an extremely tough adversary. He makes no bones about this.

- **Leverage your market position.** What Gates was unquestionably good at was leveraging Microsoft's market position to provide access to new and emerging markets. The reality is that if you own the operating system that runs on nearly every desktop computer in the world, it gives you a lot of negotiating muscle.
- **Buy expertise.** Gates' pragmatism also extended to buying his way into key markets. He has been quite prepared to go out and buy the development expertise of other companies and plug that into the Microsoft machine.
- **Keep personalities out of business decisions.** Bill Gates did not allow grudges to affect his commercial decisions. The ultimate pragmatist, on many occasions he fought a pitched battle with a rival for years, only to turn around and do business with them when it suited him.
- **Balance risk against reward.** Along with an analytical and detached approach to business, Gates was also a shrewd judge of risk, something he learnt along the way. But, where others who are risk averse have a tendency to delay decisions, Gates was only too aware that in the computer industry the speed of change is so rapid that not acting often carries the greatest risk of all.
- **Be relentless.** For over two decades Gates played poker in the most frantically competitive industry in the world. He could have retired in his thirties, a billionaire, but instead continued relentlessly to pursue his vision for the company he founded.

4

HIRE VERY SMART PEOPLE

'The deliberate way in which Gates has fashioned an organization that prizes smart people is the single most important, and deliberately overlooked, aspect of Microsoft's success.'[1]

– Randall E. Stross, business professor and author of *The Microsoft Way*

Bright as he is, Bill Gates never tried to take the credit for all of Microsoft's success. His willingness to acknowledge the talent of others in his field was crucial. As *Fortune* magazine once observed: 'Microsoft has been led by a man widely recognized as a genius in his own right, who has had the foresight to recognize the genius in others.'[2]

It's a point that Gates endorsed. 'I'd have to say my best business decisions have had to do with picking people. Deciding to go into business with Paul Allen is probably at the top of the list, and subsequently, hiring a friend – Steve Ballmer (appointed Microsoft CEO in 2000) – who has been my primary business partner ever since. It's important to have someone who you totally trust, who is totally committed, who shares your vision, and yet who has a little bit different set of skills and who also acts as something of a check on you. Some of the ideas you run by him, you know he's going to say, "Hey, wait a minute, have you thought about this and that?" The benefit of sparking off somebody who's got that kind of brilliance is that it not only makes business more fun, but it really leads to a lot of success.'[3]

Gates was never one to suffer technological fools gladly. 'I don't hire bozos', he said. In some quarters his attitude has been seen as elitist and provoked criticism. But it has a number of positive effects. The company is able to recruit many brilliant students straight from college who are attracted by the prospect of working with the very best.

WELCOME TO SMARTSVILLE

'Bill Gates embodies what was supposed to be impossible – a practical intellectual', noted Randall E. Stross. 'He consistently has sought out and hired the smartest individuals in the computer industry … and always hires the brilliant if he can. Microsoft's principal assets, in fact, are the collective craniums of Bill Gates and his employees …'.

From the start, Gates always insisted that the company required the very best minds, the 'high IQ people' in Microsoft lingo, and went out of his way to attract the very brightest recruits. 'There is no way of getting around [the fact] that in terms of IQ, you've got to be very elitist in picking the people who deserve to write software …', said Gates.[4]

When required, Gates would even personally intervene in the recruitment process. Say, for example, a particularly talented programmer needed additional persuasion to join the company, then they were likely to receive a personal call from Gates.

Stars like to work wherever the best in their field congregate. Sometimes, too, the top programmers seek out former colleagues and persuade them to join Microsoft. Back in 1981, for example, Gates recruited Charles Simonyi from Xerox PARC. Simonyi, who has been described as the 'father of Microsoft Word', in turn helped persuade others to join. 'In terms of hiring great people, how do we hire all these people? It's by word of mouth', Gates noted. 'People say it's great to work here …'.

THE ULTIMATE INTELLECTUAL CAPITALIST

In the parlance of management theory, Bill Gates has always been the ultimate intellectual capitalist. From the very start at Microsoft, for example, he knew that the company's key asset would be the calibre of its people. He consistently recruited and retained the smartest programmers, often attracting them straight from college with little or no industry experience.

> **'There is no way of getting around [the fact] that in terms of IQ, you've got to be very elitist in picking the people who deserve to write software ...'**
>
> **Bill Gates**

Business school professor Randall E. Stross likened the software business to the Hollywood movie industry. 'In the software industry, a single programmer's intellectual resources, through commercial alchemy, can create entire markets where none existed before', he said. 'Compare the cumulative worldwide gross revenues of the studio that captures the services of the next Steven Spielberg compared to the rival who has to settle for a second-round draft pick. Differences separating the rewards generated by the top tier versus the second tier are geometric, not arithmetic.'

In practice, most organizations still don't really value the talents and know-how of their employees. Those that do tend to focus on this element to the exclusion of the other dimensions of intellectual capital, such as relationships with customers and suppliers, and the whole social fabric of the organization. These are all areas where Gates has led the way.

THE CAMPUS CULTURE

At Microsoft's specially designed headquarters at Redmond, Washington, Gates deliberately set out to create an environment that suited the bright young people the company wanted to attract. With its simple aesthetics, open communal areas and green spaces, it resembled the college atmosphere familiar to many of those joining the company straight from university. Appropriately enough, it was called the Microsoft Campus (it was parodied in Douglas Coupland's 1994 novel *Microserfs*) and has grown over the years to resemble something of a sprawling unplanned suburb of its own.

Imagine carefully tended lawns surrounding wooded areas, and low-slung buildings with grey-white facing and mirrored windows nestling in-between. The original buildings were designed in the shape of an X to maximize the natural light inside. Unlike the open-plan buildings popular elsewhere in the corporate world, each office was fully enclosed with a door, and intended for one occupant.

In practice, most organizations still don't really value the talents and know-how of their employees

This was a deliberate attempt to create the sort of solitude and privacy Gates felt was necessary to allow his employees to 'sit and think' as he said he wanted them to. To ensure social interaction, the campus also included numerous cafeterias which provided food at prices subsidized by the company.

In other respects, too, the culture remained remarkably unchanged from the early days for many years. Employees dressed informally, travelled coach class and used moderately priced hotels when they travelled on business (as did Gates). There were no status symbols such as executive dining rooms or fancy office furniture.

In fact the company was built on an ethos of thrift. And, whenever employees appeared to lose sight of this ethos and were felt to be taking advantage of the company's generosity, the culture would reassert itself. Employees would be exhorted to shake off complacency: the company's success, they were reminded, had to be earned 'one day at a time'. Eating 'weenies instead of shrimp' was the path to continued success they were reminded.

Above all else, the campus atmosphere provided a pleasant working environment for Microsoft's most important employees. This was particularly important given that they were likely to spend an awful lot of time there.

CHARGE OF THE BRIGHT BRIGADE

Gates has said that the biggest factor affecting how fast Microsoft can grow has always been the availability of really smart people. To begin with he was able to recruit programmers he knew personally – 'smart friends' as he called them – but as time went on this supply ran out and he found himself having to take on 'smart strangers'.

As Gates pointed out back in the late 1990s, shortly before he appointed long time colleague and friend Steve Ballmer to the CEO spot: 'The only real disagreement Steve Ballmer [Gates' right-hand man at the time] and I ever had was when he joined the company. We had 25 people. He said, "We have to hire about 50 more people to deal with all this opportunity." I said, "No way, we can't afford it." I thought about it for a day and said, "Okay, you just hire as fast as you can, and only good people, and I'll tell you when you get ahead of the sanity picture." Here we are at 24,000 people now and still the key constraint is bringing in great people.'[5]

Despite its exponential growth, Gates always resisted the temptation to dilute the quality of Microsoft staff, especially in the product development teams. He knew that attracting the best programmers would make it much easier to recruit others of the same calibre. Other companies might put new hires on probation, but Microsoft preferred to do the close scrutiny before they were hired. Getting it right at the start avoided additional cost later, including the drop in morale that occurs when someone has to be dismissed because they aren't working out.

The company's credo on hiring people meant that a mediocre new employee was considered a worse situation than a disastrous appointment. 'We're actually OK if the person doesn't come into work', Gates explained to Microsoft managers when outlining his hiring priorities. 'But if you have somebody who's mediocre, who just sort of gets by on the job, then we're in big trouble.'

The problem, as Gates saw it, was that a mediocre employee was hard to get rid of but occupied a place in the company that could be filled by someone brilliant. To avoid this, in the early days he insisted that the company employ fewer employees than were actually required to carry out the work. His formula was n-minus-one, where n was the number of people really needed.

> **Gates always resisted the temptation to dilute the quality of Microsoft staff, especially in the product development teams**

This simple rule of thumb underlined a very clear message: hire only the very best people because your team is never going to get all the bodies you want. Right up until he handed over the day-to-day running of the business Gates ensured that Microsoft did not carry any passengers, and took a personal interest and pride in the recruitment of exceptional individuals, often interviewing them himself.

THE CAFFEINE KIDS

'I personally work long hours, but not as long as I used to. I certainly haven't expected other people to work as hard as I did. Most days I don't work more than 12 hours. On weekends I rarely work more than 8 hours. There are weekends I take off and I take vacations.'[6] One of the most quoted comments from Gates, this merely serves to underline the intensity that Gates brought the job of running the company he co-founded.

Gates' famous stamina for work translated into a Microsoft culture that can best be described as 'work hard, then work even harder'. For many years, Gates regarded taking holidays as a sign of weakness. The Microsoft campus at Redmond was geared up to allow employees to work very long hours. There are legendary tales of employee commitment in terms of the hours put in. It was certainly commonplace for Microsoft employees to have pizza delivered to their desks so that there was no need to stop working while they ate. The company put its hand in its pocket for soft drinks and coffee purchases.

In fact Microsoft has always been well known for the generous employee benefits it provides – something that has contributed to its consistently good performance in *Fortune* magazine's annual Top 100 Employer rankings – a small but important part of which is the beverage and food subsidies.[7] As one Microsoft employee once told *Newsweek*, 'Anything with caffeine is free'.

When one former Netscape employee got involved in some protracted negotiations with Microsoft he found himself doing business at what he regarded as very strange hours. 'I had numerous conversations with them very late at night, from hotel rooms across the country and from my home. The phone would ring late at night and my wife would say, "Don't tell me that's Microsoft again." It was just the Microsoft way of doing business. I don't believe they ever really sleep.'[8]

Whatever their night-time habits, Gates created a unique working environment at Redmond; at one and the same time a hothouse of creativity, yet highly efficient at project management ensuring that products were, with a few notable exceptions, delivered on time. It was to the chagrin of his rivals that the Microsoft development teams worked as well together as they did. They had a voracious appetite for work and were virtually impossible to poach; although in recent years Google has tempted some employees away from the Microsoft campus.

For many years, Gates regarded taking holidays as a sign of weakness

The ability to hold onto its staff, and attract the staff of other leading IT firms, partly by promoting a sense of shared vision and inclusiveness, is one of the secrets of Microsoft's success. 'By sharing the challenge to change the computer world with his staff Microsoft staff feel more involved with their goal than other companies because they are led by a leader who is in the trenches with them', noted *Fortune* magazine. It is an ingredient that Steve Jobs took to Apple with considerable success.

Gates also had his own particular take on managers. At Microsoft he regarded himself as an exceptional manager of people (even though some saw his aggressive and sometimes impatient style as 'management by abuse'). As a technical expert, he had little time for the notion of the generalist manager, expecting Microsoft employees to combine managerial skills with other areas of expertise.

'The art of management is to promote people without making them managers', he said once. He subsequently modified that statement by saying it was more relevant to technical environments. But views on management remained consistent.

It was to the chagrin of his rivals that the Microsoft development teams worked as well together as they did. They had a voracious appetite for work and were virtually impossible to poach

'I really don't know the difference between a professional manager and anyone else', he said. 'We're all professional, we work during the day and we get paid. Where are these non-professionals? I don't seem to see any around. We're not here to say "I'm a professional manager, give me something to manage," we're here to get the job done. So we don't actively distinguish between professional and non-professional managers.'

What the company should do is give its people very clear goals, tell them what is expected of them, and let them get on with it.

THE MICROSOFT MANAGER

Microsoft put more effort than most into defining the role of managers.

'Anyone who has people reporting to them has the word "manager" in their title', says Mike Murray, former vice president of Human Resources and the man responsible for the 'shrimp and weenie' memo. 'We expect them to get more out of their people. We have found that there are three key drivers of a successful manager at Microsoft:

- 'They make sure the group and every member in it has clear goals and objectives and performance measures.

- 'They must be very good at planning the sometimes tedious process of figuring out the details of how to get there.

- 'They give continual feedback.'

THE MILLIONAIRE CLUB

For some time Microsoft always paid its employees salaries that were lower than its rivals. That included Gates who, for many years, took an annual salary of just £175,000. What made this possible was the company's long-term commitment to stock options – offering almost all staff an 'option' to buy Microsoft shares at a fixed price in the future – a major factor in the company's ability to recruit the best programmers.

Through stock options, Bill Gates made more people millionaires than any other entrepreneur in history. As one commentator observed: 'Microsoft is singular in that its campus is a place unlike any other workplace in the world, at any other time in history, where several thousand millionaires, multimillionaires, and multi-billionaires continue to clomp to work each day.'[9]

One Wall Street firm calculated that no fewer than 2200 developers in Microsoft's Class of 1989 became millionaires in just two years. The gamble continued to pay off for successive waves of new recruits, although the halcyon years when Microsoft shares seemed to continually double in price eventually came to an end.

But, as Gates liked to remind people about his own fortune, there was always an element of risk involved. The sums were tied to the price of Microsoft shares. Sure, when the company's stock was on a seemingly endless upward spiral, then knowing when to exercise their stock options was the problem for Microsoft employees. A joke inside the company was 'there are a lot of $100,000 snowmobiles around here' – purchased for $2000 with money from selling stock options early before their value increased 50-fold. Indeed, since the turn of the century the stock price has been on a downward trend, although the share options are still an attractive benefit for potential hires.

One Wall Street firm calculated that no fewer than 2200 developers in Microsoft's Class of 1989 became millionaires in just two years

Another key aspect of Gates' approach was consistently to talk the Microsoft share price down. This was a sensible reaction to the wild fluctuations in share price that can damage the prospects of an otherwise healthy business. As Gates was well aware, high-tech companies such as Microsoft are especially vulnerable to the vagaries of Wall Street, all the more so in the lead up to the launch of strategically important new product releases such as a new version of Windows. To offset this effect, and in sharp contrast to most CEOs, Gates spent many years talking down the prospects of Microsoft.

He once noted, for example: 'We've always said that, given our long-term approach, this business will definitely go through cycles. There will be ups and downs. There haven't been any downs yet, but we are still sincere about saying that. We say our profitability, percentagewise, has grown at an unsustainable rate. We are always telling analysts, "Don't recommend our stock. We sell software, not stock. Lower your earnings estimate, be more conservative." It's not a long-term approach to promote the stock in any way.'[10]

At the time, by using the appreciation of share price as a major element of compensation, rather than merely salaries, Gates found a perfect linkage between performance and reward. As he noted: 'We're using ownership as one of the things that binds us together.'

But perhaps the most telling test of the Microsoft culture was that so many of the original employees continued to work there rather than moving on to new career challenges, and how many employees remained at the company even when they were financially secure beyond their wildest dreams.

In fact, when people did leave, then Microsoft's research suggested that it was usually because the challenge had run out.

A lot of people in their late 20s and early 30s became millionaires through taking advantage of the company's stock options. They could have easily retired, but they didn't. As one Microsoft manager put it: 'What else would they do with their lives? Where else could they have so much fun?'

That, of course, includes Gates himself, who no doubt could have retired from the day-to-day running of the business many years before he did. After all, he became a billionaire in the mid 1980s, just into his thirties.

HIRE VERY SMART PEOPLE

Gates consistently sought out and hired the smartest individuals in the computer industry. It was a deliberate strategy that ensured the company attracted the highest calibre staff. Some people accused Gates of being elitist, but he is one of the first entrepreneurs to truly understand what intellectual capital is all about.

- **Hire only the very best.** From the start, Gates always insisted that the company required the very best minds. Microsoft calls them 'high IQ people', and has gone out of its way to attract the very brightest recruits. When required Gates would intervene personally in the recruitment process.
- **Nurture creativity.** At Microsoft's specially designed headquarters at Redmond, Washington, Gates set out to create an environment which suited the bright young people the company wanted to attract. With its simple aesthetics, open communal areas and green spaces it resembled the college atmosphere familiar to many of those joining the company straight from university. Appropriately enough, it was called the Microsoft Campus.
- **Don't drop your standards.** Despite long periods of exponential growth, Gates always stoutly resisted the temptation to dilute the quality of Microsoft staff, especially in the product development teams. He realized that attracting the best programmers would make it much easier to recruit others of the same calibre.
- **Work harder than anyone else.** Gates' famous stamina for work translated into a Microsoft culture that can best be described as 'work hard, then work even harder'. For

many years, Gates regarded taking holidays as a sign of weakness. The Microsoft campus at Redmond was set up to allow employees to work very long hours, with a selection of cafeterias providing subsidized meals and soft drinks.

- **Reward employees through stock options.** In the past Microsoft has paid its employees salaries that are lower than its rivals. This was made possible by the company's long-term commitment to stock options – offering almost all staff an 'option' to buy Microsoft shares at a fixed price in the future. Through stock options, Bill Gates made more people millionaires than any other entrepreneur in history. Many of those who continue to work at the company are millionaires many times over.

5

LEARN TO SURVIVE

'Success is a lousy teacher – it seduces smart people into thinking they can't lose.'

– Bill Gates

At Microsoft Bill Gates created a voracious learning machine. Learning was a sign of a 'smart organization', Gates believed, one that is continuously improving its internal processes. It is also the best way to avoid becoming complacent, and the best protection against making mistakes. Many of his competitors were not so careful. By capitalizing on the errors of others, Gates prospered.

'Most of our success comes when we end up with a competitor who doesn't do things correctly – that's lucky. You're not supposed to work on a strategy that depends on other people's mistakes, but they've certainly made a lot', he observed.

Gates' special talent was avoiding the bear traps that others fall into, while exploiting the opportunities that arise from their mistakes. In an industry where so many of the once mighty have fallen on their faces, Gates built up an impressive track record.

In many ways, what set him apart from other leaders in the computer industry was his focus on the business. Despite his incredible success – and the distractions of fame and fortune – Gates remained as committed to Microsoft as he was at the start. He combined an analytical mind with a real passion for the technology, which meant that he was always scanning the horizon for the next big thing. This intellectual restlessness resonated throughout Microsoft. It kept Gates and his people on their toes.

NO BUGS ON US

Gates proved to be remarkably resilient in a very competitive business. In large part, this was because he stuck to what he was good at – software. At the very start when he and Paul Allen were setting up the company, it was Gates who persuaded his friend that the future was in software not hardware.

With the exception of a few distractions such as the brilliantly conceived and executed, but regrettably discontinued, Trackball Optical mouse, Gates resolutely stuck to his guns on the point, insisting that Microsoft was a software company and should retain its focus on that market. 'Microsoft is designed to write great software', he said. 'We are not designed to be good at other things. We only know how to hire, how to manage, and how to globalize software products.'[1]

> **Under Gates' influence, the company developed an impressive system of feedback loops which ensured it continuously improved everything it did**

But with Gates' acute sense of which way the tech winds were blowing, as he scanned the horizon for the next big thing, it became clear to him that multi-media convergence on non-PC platforms was seemingly unstoppable and Microsoft would have to get involved in this area. And so there have been departures into hardware territory, perhaps most notably products such as the Xbox video game console, and the Zune multimedia player.

There was a rule, too, that any bugs identified in its software had to be immediately put right. The same approach applied to the way Microsoft's internal processes were organized. Under Gates' influence, the company developed an impressive system of feedback loops which ensured it continuously improved everything it did.

MICROSOFT U

In Microsoft, Bill Gates created probably one of the few genuine learning organizations in the world. Externally the importance of learning was clearly signalled: the company headquarters in Redmond, Washington, organized along the lines of a university and even called the Microsoft Campus. But the commitment to continuous learning went much further than the physical environment.

In terms of establishing systems for retaining intellectual capital, Microsoft was a pioneer, often way ahead of the game. Many of the world's best known companies have followed suit by introducing systems for managing knowledge. But Gates always emphasized the importance of fostering a culture where knowledge is shared and retained.

Despite the apparently free and easy environment, Microsoft introduced strict rules controlling the development of its software. In particular, Gates insisted that Microsoft developers standardize their programming wherever possible – following standards that had already been developed and documented.

In this way, the development teams benefited from the work of their peers, and could move easily between projects. The alternative, as other companies have found, is a proliferation of approaches, which leads inevitably to reinventing the wheel many times over.

The company was also fanatical about learning from past mistakes. 'I used to have this memo that I updated every year called the Ten Great Mistakes of Microsoft, and I would try to make them very stimulating so people would talk about lessons for this company's future', noted Gates.

'Many of our mistakes related to markets we didn't get into as early as we should have. The constraint was always the number of people we could hire, while still managing everything, and ensuring that we could meet all of our delivery commitments. We were always on the edge. We really pushed the limits of how fast we hired people.'[2]

Being able to bring new people into the organization quickly was a key factor in the way the company developed. By creating systems for documenting knowledge, new recruits had instant access to what their colleagues had already learned. Since relatively few people actually left the company to join direct competitors, the risk of sensitive information leaving the premises was minimal. That was one reason why Gates preferred to establish Microsoft's HQ in Redmond, rather than Silicon Valley. 'They couldn't keep secrets in Silicon Valley', he observed.

Gates insisted that Microsoft developers standardize their programming wherever possible – following standards that had already been developed and documented

LOOPING THE LOOPS

At Microsoft, Gates also instituted a system where those elsewhere in the organization provide constant feedback to their colleagues. He was passionate about what he called 'feedback loops', and these were built into everything that Microsoft does.

As might be expected with one of the world's leading computing firms, Microsoft has for a long time had a highly sophisticated electronic infrastructure. Using email, anyone in the organization can communicate with anyone else – that included Gates himself.

'In a highly iterative business, where things change so rapidly, we often need to change course midstream, so we must have an efficient feedback loop', said Gates. 'Our email system, with its lack of hierarchy, ensures that everyone who needs to know about a problem is informed within 48 hours.'

Gates was famous for replying promptly to email messages from any Microsoft employee. One senior manager who left the company under a cloud is rumoured not to have checked his email often enough.

'Our email system, with its lack of hierarchy, ensures that everyone who needs to know about a problem is informed within 48 hours.'

Bill Gates

The existence of feedback loops at Microsoft also gave rise to some concerns among competitors. One area where confusion existed was with the so-called Chinese Wall between operating system development teams and applications development teams. Owning the industry standard operating system gave Microsoft's application developers a huge advantage over other software companies. In theory, Microsoft was supposed to keep the playing field level by segregating the operating systems division and the applications division. This artificial division was called the 'Chinese Wall.' However, competitors have continually argued that the wall is full of holes and that Microsoft's applications developers have inside information about the operating system that is not available to rival developers – and vice versa.

Microsoft countered this criticism by inviting software developers from other companies to Redmond for briefings about the future development of its operating system. In reality, however, it is very unlikely that any such Chinese Wall could realistically be expected to work in such a competitive industry. For one thing, it flies in the face of the concept of the learning organization. In the real world the very notion of Chinese Walls is somewhat naïve, something recognized by the antitrust settlement, which called for Microsoft to share its application programming interfaces with third-party companies, and open up other intellectual property and technical know-how.

THE LEARNING ORGANIZATION

The concept of the learning organization is based on the work of business academics Chris Argyris at Harvard Business School and Peter Senge of the Massachusetts Institute of Technology's Sloan School of Business.

'In the simplest sense, a learning organization is a group of people who are continually enhancing their capability to create their future', explains MIT's Senge, who brought the learning organization concept to a mass audience. 'The traditional meaning of the word learning is much deeper than just taking information in. It is about changing individuals so that they produce results they care about, accomplish things that are important to them.'[3]

Senge suggests there are five components to a learning organization:

1   Systems thinking – Senge champions systems thinking, recognizing that things are interconnected.

2   Personal mastery – Senge grounds this idea in the familiar competencies and skills associated with management, but also includes spiritual growth – opening oneself up to a progressively deeper reality – and living life from a creative rather than a reactive viewpoint. This discipline involves two underlying movements – continually learning how to see current reality more clearly – and the ensuing gap between vision and reality produces the creative tension from which learning arises.

3   Mental models – this essentially deals with the organization's driving and fundamental values and principles. Senge alerts managers to the power of patterns of thinking at the organizational level and the importance of non-defensive inquiry into the nature of these patterns.

4   Shared vision – here Senge stresses the importance of co-creation and argues that shared vision can only be built on personal vision. He claims that shared vision is present when the task that follows from the vision is no longer seen by the team members as separate from the self.

5   Team learning – the discipline of team learning involves two practices: dialogue and discussion. The former is characterized by its exploratory nature, the latter by the opposite process of narrowing down the field to the best alternative for the decisions that need to be made. The two are mutually complimentary, but the benefits of combining them only come from having previously separated them. Most teams lack the ability to distinguish between the two and to move consciously between them.

For the traditional company, the learning organization poses huge challenges. In the learning organization managers are researchers and designers rather than controllers and overseers. Senge argues that managers should encourage employees to be open to new ideas, communicate frankly with each other, understand thoroughly how their companies operate, form a collective vision and work together to achieve their goal.

'The world we live in presents unprecedented challenges for which our institutions are ill prepared', says Senge.[4]

CRASH TEST DUMMIES

There is one other crucial factor that has kept Microsoft at the top of its industry. Gates was always willing to test software on customers, a practice continued at Microsoft to this day. Beta versions of the company's software are offered to customers who are prepared to provide some feedback for advance knowledge of the new software. In this way, the company's developers get real feedback from the people who will use the final version of the software. Customers involved in beta testing tell the developers back in Redmond about any bugs or glitches they find, and offer input on the usability of the software.

In this way, the customer becomes part of the feedback process even before the product has been launched, something that speeds up market acceptance of new products. It is also a major factor in the speed with which Microsoft can develop and market new applications.

Critics argue that by releasing applications before they have been properly tested, Microsoft actually uses its customers as crash test dummies. However, many of the companies that get involved see it as a useful exercise to gain advance information about future Microsoft developments, and even to influence the final product.

Many high-tech companies have a vested interest in future Microsoft releases because the software and systems they produce are reliant on Microsoft software. They benefit from advance information from the company's development teams about the direction that technology is moving in – a factor that can make an important difference to the success of their own future products.

KNOW THYSELF

'If Hewlett-Packard knew what it knows we'd be three times more productive', Lew Platt, former chief executive of the US computer giant, once observed. And H-P isn't the only major corporation company that has been keen to embrace the latest panacea for business success. Xerox, Unilever, GE, Unisys, Motorola, these are just some of the many other serious-minded companies that have wrestled with the thorny issue of knowledge management.

Microsoft has been practising knowledge management for years. It is linked to the broader issue of intellectual capital (IC). Intellectual capital, in turn, is usually divided into three categories: 'human capital', 'customer capital' and 'structural capital'. Human capital is what's inside employees' heads, customer capital is to do with customer relationships, but structural capital is knowledge that is retained within the organization and can be passed on to new employees. It is this third category that is the key to knowledge management.

Thomas A. Stewart, Chief Marketing and Knowledge Officer of Booz & Company, the management consultants, author of *Intellectual Capital: The New Wealth of Organizations* (1997) and *Wealth of Knowledge: Intellectual Capital and the Twenty-first Century Organization* is a well respected expert on the subject: 'Structural capital is knowledge that doesn't go home at night.' It includes all sorts of elements including processes, systems and policies that represent the accumulation of the organization's experience over its lifetime.

**'If Hewlett-Packard knew what it knows we'd be three times more productive'
Lew Platt**

Knowledge management is largely about trying to transform the other two types of intellectual capital into structural capital. The idea is that competitive advantage can be gained from know-how that can be captured, catalogued and made available to everyone. Through its continuous feedback loops and the standardization of programming code, Microsoft has always been good at knowledge management.

KNOWLEDGE MANAGEMENT STRUCTURE (KMS)

The Knowledge Management Structure (KMS) is a term put forward by management writer Tom Peters as a development of the learning organization. The 'new' firm must destroy bureaucracy but needs to nurture knowledge and skill, Peters says, building expertise in ways that enhance the power of market-scale units, and that encourage those units to contribute knowledge for the benefit of the firm as a whole. Microsoft is made up of KMSs.

LEARN TO SURVIVE

In Microsoft, Bill Gates created a voracious learning machine, the sign of a 'smart organization', and the only way to avoid making the same mistake twice. His competitors have not always been as careful. In part, Microsoft has prospered by capitalizing on the mistakes of others.

- **Stick to the knitting.** Gates proved remarkably resilient in a very competitive business. In large part this was because, for a very long time, he stuck to what he was good at – software.
- **Create a learning organization.** In Microsoft, Bill Gates created one of the first genuine learning organizations in the world. The company's headquarters in Redmond, Washington, is organized along the lines of a university and is even called the Microsoft Campus.
- **Create continuous feedback loops.** At Microsoft, Gates instituted a system where those elsewhere in the organization provide constant feedback to their colleagues. Passionate about what he calls 'feedback loops', Gates built them into everything that Microsoft does.
- **Test your products on real customers.** Gates was always willing to test software with customers. Beta versions of the company's software are offered to customers who are prepared to provide some feedback for advance knowledge of the new software. In this way, the company's developers get real feedback from the people who will use the final version of the software.
- **Know thyself.** Today, knowledge management is all the rage with business school professors and management gurus. Initiated by Gates relentless quest for knowledge, Microsoft has been doing it for years.

6

DON'T EXPECT ANY THANKS

'Essentially, we have two choices. On the one hand, we can accept a characterization of Gates as the antichrist, Microsoft as the evil empire, its software as junk, and the company's success as rooted in deceptions, outright lies, legal trickery, and brute-force marketing. On the other hand, we can take the company at its own word that it has benevolently ushered in the personal computer revolution and that its market success is the just reward for the service it has rendered the public.'[1]

– Randall E. Stross, *The Microsoft Way*

If there is one lesson that Bill Gates has learned the hard way it is that being famous and being infamous are closely linked. You can't expect to become the richest man in the world without making some enemies – and in the computer industry Gates made more than his share of those. He also attracted the interest of anti-trust authorities, both in the US and Europe, who have questioned whether some of Microsoft's business practices are anti-competitive for many years.

At the same time, being incredibly rich and successful also brings its share of sycophants. The wealthy and the famous, the politicians and the Hollywood movie moguls all courted Gates and his Microsoft executives. Most of those who beat a path to his door wanted to meet Gates or one of his right-hand men to discuss the digital future and the possibilities of collaborating with Microsoft.

Over the years, too, Gates has shown that he understands the importance of having friends in high places. Despite his long running battle with the US antitrust regulators, he courted the CEOs of Fortune 500 companies, conducting CEO forums in Seattle and other cities across the US, and held discussions with the heads of a number of European companies.

Yet for all the publicity he attracted, Gates was – and remains – fiercely protective of his private life, which he does not consider a matter of public interest. It is a rather naïve attitude. Not only is he co-founder of one of the most powerful companies in the world – and one that, on a daily basis, is changing the way people live their lives, he is also the richest man in the world. When you add in his celebrated intellect, his reputation for tantrums, and his decision to spend $50 million plus on a mansion just outside Seattle, then it becomes clear that his every move is going to be closely watched by the world's media.

BILLION DOLLAR BILL

Bill Gates has always had a love/hate relationship with the media. On the one hand, he seemed to enjoy the attention that greeted his every pronouncement on the future of technology. But he also seemed genuinely mystified by the negative publicity that Microsoft attracted during his tenure as CEO.

In countries outside of the US, a visit by Gates was often afforded the same sort of attention as a visit by a head of government, and indeed despite his shift away from Microsoft responsibilities, it often still is. Politicians still love to be photographed in his company. And if Microsoft doesn't benefit quite so much from this publicity these days, it certainly used to.

Despite his long running battle with the US antitrust regulators, he courted the CEOs of Fortune 500 companies, conducting CEO forums in Seattle and other cities across the US, and held discussions with the heads of a number of European companies

'The amount of press attention is not consistently linked to size: Microsoft and its chairman receive attention that exceeds all personal computer companies combined', notes Randall E. Stross. 'Even though in 1996, Intel's earnings were exactly double those of Microsoft – $3.6 billion versus $1.8 billion, ranking Intel seventh in highest profits of all corporations versus Microsoft's position of 29th.'

The somewhat overdue launch of Windows 95, for example, was one of the most written about events in commercial history. The launch of Vista in January 2007 was blogged live around the world and was still kicked off by Gates, despite his reduction of duties. Of course there is a downside to all that oxygen of publicity; the media is all over you if you get it wrong.

MESSIAH OR ANTICHRIST?

The most startling aspect of the publicity that surrounded Bill Gates when he was running Microsoft, and still does to a degree was its intensity. For some reason, to a large number of people Bill Gates came to epitomize the sinister machinations of big business in a way that no other businessman ever did before.

In April 1996, for example, *Wired* magazine supplied its readers with a tourist guide to the world wide web entitled 'On hating Microsoft'. Every site listed was devoted to venting anger and other strong negative sentiments about Microsoft and Gates. One site, proclaiming itself the 'Bill Gates Fun Page', offered a photograph of the Microsoft CEO with two Devil's horns added to his head. Gates haters were directed to choose from a selection of lethal weapons including a knife, a handgun, and an Uzi machine gun, that could be turned on his image by a simple click of the mouse. Weird as it is, this was just one of the many bizarre forms that anti-Microsoft sentiment has taken over the years.

Although sentiments have improved since he began battling the world's ills via his philanthropic endeavours, social historians might one day be able to explain why so many people disliked him so much. For now, we can only speculate on the reasons. The most obvious explanation is envy. A lot of people resent the fact that Bill Gates has made so much money and they have not. It may be that simple. But more likely, there are a number of factors.

Is it pure coincidence, for example, that the rise of the 'Bill Gates as Antichrist' movement mirrored the decline of another US bogey-man, the Reds under the beds? With the unravelling of the Russian communist empire, there were vacancies for new villains out to get hard-working, ordinary Americans, and for a new evil empire. Who better to fuel the conspiracy theories than an incredibly rich and powerful computer nerd at the head of a global software company? Bill Gates, come on down.

Gates is not the first mega-rich tycoon in American history to be vilified for anti-competitive activities. A century ago, the Texas oil baron John D. Rockefeller gained control of America's refinery business and oil pipelines. Rockefeller then leveraged that power into control of oil production. Critics of Bill Gates say DOS was the equivalent of a pipeline and its ownership gave Gates the control of the entire industry.

A lot of people resent the fact that Bill Gates has made so much money and they have not

On the other side, there is an equally passionate, if much smaller, group that seems to credit Gates with almost godly powers. For these people, he is the golden boy, whose incredible intellect and visionary powers made him the closest thing the world has had to a technology oracle. When Gates pronounced on the future – be it the likely convergence of technology, the spread of new software applications, or the shake up of the video games market – there were always plenty of people in high places who sat up and listened (notwithstanding the fact that he didn't always get it right).

If there is a lesson in all of this, it has to be that when you've got as much money as Bill Gates there is no way that you're going to please everyone – and it's pointless trying. This is certainly something Gates seems to have realized over the years.

CORPORATE BOGEYMEN

It is not the first time that America's thirst for a villain has found a soft target in a hugely rich business tycoon. The reclusive oil baron

John D. Rockefeller, and J.P. Morgan, the king of Wall Street, both became bogeymen for the failings of the industrial age.

Teddy Roosevelt built a political career that took him all the way to the White House on trust-busting. He was the first to use the Sherman Act, the basis for the case against Gates, when he went after Morgan in 1902. The act had been drawn up 12 years earlier in response to the monopoly positions of Rockefeller's Standard Oil and others. In 1911, it led to the breaking up of Standard Oil into a string of smaller companies. Ironically, this actually made Rockefeller even richer. The same legislation was invoked years later against Ma Bell. In the 1970s IBM was also investigated, with some calling for the dismantling of Big Blue into a series of Little Blues.

So Microsoft too has had its turn, with Gates as Public Enemy Number 1 (who knows, maybe Google will one day supplant Microsoft as the target of people's IT ire). On one point at least Randall Stross was right beyond any shadow of a doubt: the strength of anti-Gates/Microsoft feeling presents a very odd – and possibly unique – phenomenon. It is hard to identify any other company or businessman who has ever provoked such deep distrust.

TECHNO TYRANT

On a personal level, too, Bill Gates has sometimes been described in less than glowing terms. As a child he had a tendency to temper tantrums – a habit some of those who've worked with him say he hasn't lost. Certainly Gates has not suffered fools gladly.

'Time is very short, so if people are repeating things that I already know or if they aren't smart or didn't listen to something that I said with some precision, then that's not a good person for me to work with – they don't belong in this team', he once said. His own intellect makes him impatient of those who aren't as smart as him.

It has been remarked that his social skills are not as developed as his other faculties. In reality, Gates is the product of his experiences as much as anyone else. A precocious and highly intelligent child, he went on to attend an elite secondary school before taking up a place at America's most famous university. He went to Harvard, he said, to learn from people smarter than he was … and was disappointed.[2]

Gates has spent his whole life among very smart people and has had a low tolerance for those whose intellect he does not respect. At company briefings he has been known to go ballistic, throwing things and shouting 'this is the stupidest thing I've ever heard of …', a familiar phrase to people who work with him.

> **'Time is very short, so if people are repeating things that I already know or if they aren't smart or didn't listen to something that I said with some precision, then that's not a good person for me to work with – they don't belong in this team'**
> **Bill Gates**

You could argue that if he behaves like a spoilt child then he really doesn't deserve to be liked. But there is another side to Gates. He can be charming – if not quite charismatic. He has also demonstrated on numerous occasions while at Microsoft that he can be extremely patient when an important deal is at stake. The poker-playing days at Harvard stood him in good stead. His cool, analytical mind made him a better strategist than most of his rivals. And, as his more recent activities with the Bill & Melinda Gates Foundation have shown, he has been able to use the resourcefulness he acquired during his days at Microsoft to good effect. Tackling global challenges such as malaria, HIV and tuberculosis makes Gates Mk2 look like a downright good guy.

Not that there weren't signs of his generosity of spirit during the Microsoft golden years.

Indeed, on the day that Windows 95 'went golden' – i.e. no more changes would be made in the code before it was shipped – Gates sent a truckload of chilled Dom Perignon and several cases of whipped cream to the programmers who had been working around the clock. 'You give 450 geeks champagne and whipped cream and it's an ugly sight', observed the team leader, as his colleagues let off steam.

At one level, Gates was simply behaving like a brat when he threw his weight around. But then if you are the richest man in the world, and a genius to boot, that's only to be expected. Journalists who interviewed him were lucky if they didn't ask something that Gates regards as a 'stupid question'. There are many signs, however, that the techno-tyrant has mellowed with age. Some say that marriage calmed his temper, and that his friendship with the philosophical investment guru Warren Buffett also helped to make him more relaxed about life.

BILL AND WARREN'S EXCELLENT ADVENTURE

When Bill Gates and investment sage Warren Buffett said they were taking a vacation together in China in 1995, many in the media thought it had to be some kind of weird publicity stunt. Commentators wondered what the world's two richest men could possibly have in common besides their cash mountains.

Buffett (born 1930) has described himself as a 'cyber-idiot' who avoids investing in high-tech companies like Microsoft because he doesn't understand them. Gates was known to have a short fuse and to be impatient with people not conversant with the ins and outs of software design. It was – and in some ways remains – an odd friendship, then, but it certainly seems to have blossomed over the years as the two vie for the title of richest man in the world. (Gates is still nudging it, especially as Buffett has had a bad time investment-wise in the recent financial crisis.)

'We went to China for a lot of reasons', Gates said. 'Partly to relax and have fun. We found a few McDonalds there, so we didn't feel too far away from home. It was also exciting to go and see all the changes taking place, to see different parts of the country, and to meet some of the leaders.'

But the trip was more than a vacation for the two buddies. As ever, Gates had his eye on the bottom line. 'China is a market that Microsoft had already been investing in', he said at the time. 'We've upped that a lot since then. As a percentage of our sales, though, it's tiny – well under 1% – and so even though it will double every year for the next five years, it's really only by taking a ten-year view that we can say it's worth the emphasis we're putting on it.

'Although about three million computers get sold every year in China, people don't pay for the software. Someday they will, though. And as long as they're going to steal it, we want them to steal ours. They'll get sort of addicted, and then we'll somehow figure out how to collect sometime in the next decade.'

And, as usual, with the Chinese market Gates seemed to win out where many other corporations had failed. So much so that by the summer of 2007 *Fortune* magazine published an article titled: 'How Microsoft conquered China'.

'Although about three million computers get sold every year in China, people don't pay for the software. Someday they will, though. And as long as they're going to steal it, we want them to steal ours.'

Bill Gates

Buffett, too, was impressed with the potential of the Chinese domestic market, noting that the Chinese would buy an awful lot of Coca-Cola. The two have been firm friends ever since and have spent several subsequent vacations and weekends together.

In 1998, they got together to give what was at the time a rare public appearance, sharing the stage for a 90-minute question and answer session on their business philosophies. The event, held at the University Of Washington, near Gates' headquarters at Redmond, caused such a stir that the queue of buck-struck students stretched through the lobby and out the door of the union building in Seattle.

The billionaire buddies make an odd couple. Yet they get on like long-lost friends. On the occasion in question, the superinvestor and the cybertycoon invited 350 business school students to participate by asking a series of questions.

So what did this great meeting of minds reveal to the assembled audience? The $64,000 question – or, to be more precise, the multi-billion dollar question, as that is what Gates and Buffett are believed to be worth – was just how did they get to be so rich?

The two multi-billionaires were surprisingly frank. Buffett put his own financial success down not to his IQ but to 'rationality'. Anyone could do what he had done, he said with disarming disingen-uousness; all they had to do was develop the right habits. That meant adopting the habits of those they admired and rejecting the habits of those they despised. He had turned down deals with people he didn't like, he said. The important thing was to enjoy what you did.

Gates agreed with both points. His own habits, he admitted, had been formed by an early exposure to computers and the company of fellow computer fanatics. What he really enjoyed was solving problems.

They must have enjoyed the experience though, as they recon-vened for Buffett's home fixture at the University of Nebraska at Lincoln's College of Business Administration in 2005 (more of which later). And, at the time of writing, both were due to do a star turn as the 'Big Men on Campus' event held at Columbia Business School (where Buffett once studied), fielding questions from busi-ness school students in front of the CNBC cameras.

DON'T EXPECT ANY THANKS

If there is one lesson that Bill Gates learned the hard way it is that fame and infamy are never far apart. You can't expect to become the richest man in the world without making some enemies. Working in the computer industry Gates got more than his share of those. What it taught him was:

- **Don't let jealousy faze you.** The most startling aspect of the publicity that has surrounded Bill Gates is its intensity. For some reason, to a large number of people Gates came to epitomize the sinister machinations of big business in a way that no other businessman has ever done before. His reaction was to defend himself with reasoned argument.

- **Use media attention to market your products.** Microsoft benefits from the publicity surrounding its famous founder. When Gates went to countries outside of the US as CEO of Microsoft, he was often afforded the same sort of attention as a visiting head of state. It gave Gates unrivalled access to the corridors of power.

- **Don't suffer fools.** Gates has spent his whole life among very smart people. He has a low tolerance for 'stupid' questions. As a counterpoint, critics argued that his social skills would benefit from some polish. But if he was brusque or reticent, it doesn't seem to have done him any harm.

- **Hang out with the rich and popular.** When Bill Gates and investment guru Warren Buffett said they were taking a vacation together in China in 1995, many in the media thought it had to be some kind of weird publicity stunt. Commentators wondered what the world's two richest men could possibly have in common besides their cash mountains. Gates and Buffett have turned out to be firm friends. Some of Buffett's popularity has rubbed off on Gates.

7

ASSUME THE VISIONARY POSITION

'The only big companies that succeed will be those that obsolete their own products before somebody else does.'

– Bill Gates

When Bill Gates emerged onto the global CEO stage it was clear that he was a new type of business leader. Over the years, he repeatedly demonstrated that he was the closest thing the computer industry had to a seer. His in-depth understanding of technology and unique way of synthesizing data gave him a special ability to spot future trends (with one notable exception – the Internet) and steer Microsoft's strategy. This inspired awe among Microsoft fans and intimidated competitors. (Gates himself was always dismissive of the visionary role. 'Vision is free. And it's therefore not a competitive advantage any way, shape or form', is a typical Gatesism.)

But Gates also fulfilled another important role at Microsoft. He was the custodian of the company's culture and values. Some companies, such as Google have a clearly stated mission statement 'to organize the world's info and make it universally accessible and useful'. Others documented their values in books – Johnson & Johnson, for example, had its values written down in the Credo – which dates back to the founding fathers of the company. The founders of Hewlett-Packard created the H-P Way, which was then written out by hand and pinned up by employees next to the pictures of their family and pets.

Microsoft's mission was elegantly precise: 'a computer on every desk and in every home'. The company didn't have carved words in stone, or the corporate equivalent of the US Declaration of Independence, instead it had Bill Gates, the company's resident luminary and global IT guru.

In the mid-to-late 1990s he took this one step further by writing about the future of technology both in *The Road Ahead* and *Business @ the Speed of Thought*. This was a somewhat risky strategy, but Gates obviously felt obliged to live up to his image as the computer visionary.

SITTING AND THINKING

Today, many companies are moving away from hierarchical command-and-control management structures. Leading the way in this movement towards more decentralized structures have been the high-tech companies, which rely on knowledge workers such as software designers to carry out their work unsupervised. Microsoft was in the vanguard of this movement.

Gates said that he paid his people to 'sit and think'. But even more than the Microsoft programmers, Gates himself regarded his role as that of the company's visionary. He was dismissive of the more mundane aspects of running a business, believing that his job was to chart the future.

Gates' own talent is for understanding what's just around the corner; it is a talent still evident as he assesses the threats to global society and apportions his philanthropic dollars accordingly

'How do you manage the sales force and make sure that those measurement systems are really tracked down to the individual level to encourage the right behaviour? I'll sit in meetings where Steve Ballmer talks about how he wants to do it, but that's not my expertise. How do we advertise to get these messages across? I sort of know where we are going long-term. I've got to make sure people are coming up with messages consistent with that future. But I'm not expert in those things.'[1]

What he did regard himself to be an expert in at Microsoft was unravelling the technological past from the technological future. Gates' own talent is for understanding what's just around the corner; it is a talent still evident as he assesses the threats to global society and apportions his philanthropic dollars accordingly. His great talent as a hi-tech leader lay in his ability to inspire the people that surrounded him to meet the challenge of helping him transform the computer industry.

Over the years, he made his role within Microsoft more explicit, responding to his own brief to 'establish how things should get done'. 'I'm in the leadership role', he explained, 'so generally that means working with the developers to ensure we're doing the right things, working with the right products and key customers'. The ultimate expression of how Gates perceived his role at Microsoft came when he assumed the title of Chief Software Architect in 2000, while handing over the CEO title.

RAM RAIDER

Despite Gates' reputation as a visionary, a criticism often made of Microsoft was that the company was not a great innovator, and simply raided the ideas of others – converting them into Microsoft products. Windows, Microsoft's PC operating system, for example, is still seen by many as an imitation of Apple's Macintosh software.

The company has also been accused of a predatory attitude towards its partners. Microsoft has been described as 'the fox that takes you across the river and then eats you'.[2] But according to one industry insider, most of the criticism is sour grapes on the part of its competitors.

'Like the Japanese computer companies, Microsoft may not be an inventor, but it perfects products', said Richard Shaffer, president of industry consulting group Technologic in the days before it was acquired by Dow Jones Newsletters.[3]

Gates also showed that he was good at fostering innovation, and created a culture at Microsoft that tolerated eccentric behaviour from creative employees. One software designer at Microsoft, for example, filled his workspace with soft toys. Colleagues knew if they saw him clutching a teddy bear under one arm then he was having a tough day and should be approached with caution.

MANAGING CREATIVITY

The actual management processes involved in channelling creative people has always been something of a mystery both to management academics and business. There has been the occasional academic insight into how to herd the creative cats in organizations. Not least the research project carried out by John Whatmore at the Roffey Park Management Institute in the UK, which looked at how leaders of creative teams got the best from the special talents at their disposal.

'Like the Japanese computer companies, Microsoft may not be an inventor, but it perfects products', Richard Shaffer, former president of Technologic

Researchers put creative teams from fields including improvisational theatre, drug research, sport, theatre, film and journalism under the microscope. 'Creative people are often seen as difficult or impossible to manage', said Whatmore, 'but it is clear that some people have a gift for getting the best from the talent available, and even for getting more out of creative people than they thought they had to give. It often requires a different style of management – "a lightness of touch on the reins".'

The research indicated that people who excel at leading creative teams foster an environment conducive to innovation and which is supportive of the aspirations of the individuals involved. They also have their own ways of nudging people to get the best ideas – or as one leader put it, of 'tickling their thinking'.

People who do it well have a number of common characteristics; the research suggests that:

- they are often gregarious individuals, with the ability to stimulate ideas by expressing the same issue in different ways;

- they have the ability to read others, a skill which enables them to push the right buttons to get their best performance;

- they understand the interplay between creativity and criticism, setting up 'creative tensions' between team members and providing constant feedback; and

- they are adept at promoting social interaction between team members – often through informal meetings outside of work.

Beyond these personal skills, they have a vision of what can be achieved, based on a broad technical understanding of the field. They select team members with complementary differences, taking account not just of technical expertise but of the mix of personalities and give them a great deal of freedom, and they shield the team from external pressures from other parts of the organization.

Findings from the study suggest that effective leaders of creative groups do five critical things:

1   they give members of the team a great deal of freedom;

2   they encourage them to approach issues as a team to maxi-
     mize the creative energy focused on any given problem;

3   they give support to individual members, particularly in the
     period after a failure;

4   they give extensive responsibility to individuals, allowing
     them to decide not just how they will do a task but the tasks
     they choose to do; and

5   they shield the team from external pressures from other
     departments.

But these elements are important to different people in different
ways.

'Take freedom, for example', Whatmore explained, 'it's a wonderful metaphor for experimentation. There is the freedom to do what
interests you, the freedom to start work at midnight, the freedom to
back your own hunch and, of course, the freedom to be wrong.'

NERD INSTINCT

Gates always spoke the language of computer programmers. Programming was in his blood after all. Programming pervaded his
everyday speech. He talked frequently about 'maximum bandwidth', and even nicknamed one girlfriend '32-bit'. This was both
one of his great strengths as a leader and also one of his great
weaknesses. Talking to fellow techies, it gave him an open channel of communication allowing him to inspire Microsoft employ-

ees to greater heights. On the negative side, however, his nerdy vocabulary and directness could make him seem inarticulate when he tried to communicate to the wider public.

Gates' own direct, slightly impatient manner and his unwillingness to suffer fools also made him appear rude. On a good day he was charming, but on a bad day downright abrasive. At industry gatherings he could seem condescending – even patronizing – about the ideas of others. At internal meetings he was prone to outbursts – some say tantrums – if he didn't like the way the discussion was moving.

'That is the stupidest idea I've ever heard', was a typical Gates line. Direct, but hardly likely to make the person he's talking to inclined to volunteer more ideas. Steve Ballmer, a long-term Gates aide and friend for more than 20 years was well aware of how the Microsoft CEO came across sometimes.

'Part of Bill's style of presenting, clarifying and challenging ideas is to be very blunt, and a little bit dramatic and some would say a little rude', he said. 'But he is a lot less rude than he was 10 years ago.'[4]

Like all his other challenges Gates worked hard on his presentational skills over the years. So much so that by 2009 he was being held up as an exemplar of how to deliver effective presentations. For example, in Simon Mair and Jeremy Kourdi's *The 100: Insights and lessons from 100 of the greatest speeches ever delivered*, the authors take note of Gates' relaxed style and sincerity. In particular they highlight a number of best practice points about Gates' speechmaking:

- he is slow, focused, relaxed and casual, but still engaging;

- he establishes rapport quickly, includes both moments of levity and moments of seriousness, and has a personal touch;

- he is approachable, standing in front of the lectern removing the barrier between him and the audience; and

- he speaks gently but still shows powerful emotion.

LEADERSHIP BY STORYTELLING

'Effective leaders recognize that the ultimate test of leadership is sustained success, which demands the constant cultivation of future leaders', says Noel Tichy of the University of Michigan.[5] Leaders must, therefore, invest in developing the leaders of tomorrow and they must communicate directly to those who will follow in their footsteps.

'Part of Bill's style of presenting, clarifying and challenging ideas is to be very blunt, and a little bit dramatic and some would say a little rude ... But he is a lot less rude than he was 10 years ago.'
Steve Ballmer

Tichy believes that being able to pass on leadership skills to others requires three things. First, a *teachable point of view*: 'You must be able to talk clearly and convincingly about who you are, why you exist and how you operate.' Second, *the leader requires a story*. 'Dramatic storytelling is the way people learn from one another', Tichy writes, suggesting that this explains why Bill Gates and the like feel the need to write books. The third element in passing on the torch of leadership is *teaching methodology*: 'To be a great teacher you have to be a great learner.' The great corporate leaders are hungry to know more and do not regard their knowledge as static or comprehensive.

THE PARANOID PROPHET

It was another Silicon Valley visionary, Andy Grove of Intel, who coined the phrase 'Only the paranoid survive' as the title to his book. But it could just as well have been Bill Gates. 'The more successful I am', Gates noted, 'the more vulnerable I feel'.

It is an indication of the nature of the computer industry that two such successful business leaders should subscribe to a business creed of perpetual paranoia. But it is hardly surprising given the speed of change within their markets. What these two modern business leaders recognize is that in their particular businesses, change is a given.

From the very beginning, despite its near miraculous profit margins, Gates always worried about Microsoft's financial situation. 'Even though if you look back and see that our sales and profits grew by basically 50 percent a year for all those years, what I really remember is worrying all the time. If you ask about a specific year, I'd tell you, oh that was an awful year, we had to get Multiplan [a financial spreadsheet] out and establish it, or that was the terrible year we brought out a Microsoft mouse and it didn't sell so we had a warehouse full of them, or that was the miserable year we hired a guy to be president who didn't work out.'[6]

The more established you are, therefore, the more vulnerable your position. The problem for the market leader in an industry that is in a constant state of revolution is that you can be top dog one day and find yourself completely stranded the next because you didn't take heed of some change in direction.

The need to spot paradigm changes is most evident with high-tech companies. No one knows this better than Bill Gates. After all, it was precisely this sort of paradigm change that caught IBM napping and meant that it handed him the operating systems market on a plate – which in turn proved to be the dominant position in the software market. For this reason, Microsoft has behaved at times almost as if it has multiple personalities, pursuing several different and even conflicting technologies, for fear of backing the wrong horse. As its chief lookout and self-appointed visionary, Gates had the unenviable task of scanning the horizon for the next big thing. Sometimes even he missed something big.

> **'The more successful I am, the more vulnerable I feel.'**
> **Bill Gates**

Even after he had run the business for years, Gates admitted to being driven by a 'latent fear' that the company could become complacent and allow itself to be overtaken by nimbler competitors. 'Every company is going to have to avoid business as usual. The only big companies that succeed will be those that obsolete their own products before somebody else does', he said.[7]

STRATEGIC INFLEXION POINTS

In his book *Only The Paranoid Survive*, Intel's Andy Grove talks about 'strategic inflexion points'. These, he says, occur when a company's competitive position goes through a transition. It is the point at which the organization must alter the path it is on – adapting itself to the new situation – or it risks going into decline.

'During a strategic inflexion point the way a business operates, the very structure and concept of the business, undergoes a change', he says. 'But the irony is that at that point itself nothing much happens. That subtle point is like the eye of a hurricane. There is no wind at the eye of the hurricane, but when it moves the wind hits you again.

'That is what happens in the middle of the transformation from one business model to another. The irony is that, even though these are the most cataclysmic changes that a business can undertake, more often than not those changes are missed.'

As Sir Peter Job, the former chief executive of Reuters, the news and financial information giant once noted, when a new paradigm like the Internet is in the offing there is no time for hesitation. 'At those times', he says, 'it's important to leave your strategy suitcase in the station and catch the train'.

BETTER LATE THAN NEVER

In the early days of the Internet, dark clouds appeared to be gathering over Redmond as prophets of doom predicted that the Internet could be Microsoft's undoing. Gates, they said, had been caught napping by the rapid advance of the Internet and how it would transform the PC software industry. Some even drew parallels with IBM which lost its way at the beginning of the 1980s with the switch from mainframes to PCs. The chief beneficiary then was one, Bill Gates.

The Internet still could be Microsoft's undoing, of course, but probably not anytime soon. Critics argued, with some reason, that Microsoft's illustrious leader seemed unusually blind to the potential of the Internet for home users – even a step behind other people at Microsoft. Although a long delay in latching on to the possibilities of the Internet, or pursuing the wrong strategy, could have cost the company dearly, the penny dropped for Gates, and Microsoft had the resources to play some serious catch-up.

Gates embraced the Superhighway with the zeal of a convert. 'The Internet is not a fad in any way. It is a fantastic thing; it makes software and computers more relevant', he belatedly proclaimed.[8] Gates fans say this actually shows great strength of character, that his willingness to make a U-turn of this kind is characteristic of the sort of leadership demanded in the modern business world.

There is even academic theory to support this idea (or perhaps management theorists were simply trying to unravel the leadership style of Bill Gates). Charles Schwenk, now retired from his position as a professor of Management at the Kelly School of Business, Indiana University, contended that the call from management thinkers for strong visions could be the first step towards corporate totalitarianism.[9]

Schwenk believes that decision making should build from diversity of opinion rather than a simplistic statement of corporate intent. This requires 'weaker leadership' and that 'top management's vision is less clearly communicated (and less strongly enforced) than the advocates of management vision recommend'.

He pointed to the example of Microsoft's slow endorsement of the Internet. Originally, the Internet was not looked upon as fertile ground. Bill Gates' apparently all-encompassing vision did not include entering the Internet fray. Eventually, after much internal lobbying, Gates changed his mind and the company moved into Internet services. By traditional yardsticks this was an act of weak leadership. Visions are worthless if they are so easily changed.

The Internet still could be Microsoft's undoing, of course, but probably not anytime soon

Surrender is not in the vocabulary of the John Wayne type leader. Think again. What if Gates was wrong? Should a single view of the future always prevail? Schwenk thinks not: 'Without tolerance for eccentricity it is unlikely that any technique for encouraging the expression of diverse views will improve decision making in a firm.'

Others would argue that the Internet example simply shows that even Gates can get it wrong sometimes. The fact is that he has tended to get a lot more right than wrong over the years.

UNIQUE FORESIGHT

'The question for companies today is how do you create strategy in the absence of a map? IBM didn't wake up one morning and take a stupid pill. It didn't have implementation problems in the 1980s; it had foresight problems ten years earlier.'

So says Gary Hamel, visiting professor of Strategic and International Management at London Business School, and co-author of *Competing for the Future*, the book that established the term 'core competencies' in the business lexicon. Unique foresight, according to Hamel, is the key to strategy that works. The goal is not to predict what may happen but 'to figure out the future you can make happen. It's about winning by changing the rules of the game.' In the past, this is something that Bill Gates has excelled at.

But according to Hamel, in future, companies don't need leaders with big ideas. 'The next phase is to move to non-linear strategies', he says, 'strategies that represent a quantum leap. They will not be created by the guys at the top of the company.'

'Yesterday's visionary is today's straightjacket', he says. 'Look at how Microsoft responded to the Internet. Bill Gates was the last person in the company to get it.'

What companies need, he says, is to hear new voices. In many organizations the conversations about the future are the same people having the same conversations. Over time you get a lack of genetic diversity. It's ironic that in most companies young people who are its future are disenfranchised from the debate.

'Organizations need a hierarchy of imagination not of experience. They don't need visionaries, they need activists.'

ASSUME THE VISIONARY POSITION

Bill Gates was one of the first of a new type of business leader. Over the years, he repeatedly demonstrated that he was the closest thing the computer industry has to a seer. His in-depth understanding of technology and unique way of synthesizing data gave him a special ability to spot future trends and steer Microsoft's strategy. This also inspired awe among Microsoft fans and intimidated competitors.

- **Sit and think.** Gates paid his people to 'sit and think', he said. And Gates regarded his own role as that of the company's visionary. Dismissive of the more mundane aspects of running a business, he believed that his job was to chart the future.

- **Adopt and adapt.** A criticism that has often been made of Microsoft is that the company is not a great innovator, and simply raids the ideas of others. But there is no question that the company is good at recognizing the commercial potential of ideas and marketing them.

- **Speak the language.** Gates spoke the language of computer programmers. It was one of his great strengths as a leader and also one of his great weaknesses. Talking to fellow techies gave him an open channel of communication which allowed him to inspire Microsoft employees to greater heights. On the negative side, however, his nerdy vocabulary and directness made him seem inarticulate at times when trying to communicate with a wider public.

- **Watch your back.** Gates said he was driven by a 'latent fear' that the company could become complacent and allow itself to be overtaken by nimbler competitors. 'Every company is going to have to avoid business as usual. The only big companies that succeed will be those that obsolete their own products before somebody else does.'[10]

- **Better late than never.** Critics argued that Microsoft's illustrious leader was the last person at Microsoft to see the potential of the Internet for home users. This could have cost the company dearly. But fortunately, when the penny finally dropped for Gates, Microsoft had the resources to play some serious catch-up. 'The Internet is not a fad in any way', Gates said. 'It is a fantastic thing; it makes software and computers more relevant.'

8
COVER ALL THE BASES

'If you sit still, the value of what you have drops to zero pretty quickly.'

– Bill Gates[1]

A key element of Microsoft's success is its ability to manage a large number of projects simultaneously. Gates was considered the original multitasking man, and is said to be able to hold several different technical conversations simultaneously.

He refers to unused mental capacity as 'unused bandwidth', and has deployed a number of techniques to ensure that his own is kept to a minimum. These have included posting maps on ceilings and taking copies of *The Economist* and scientific journals to read when he meets friends for lunch. His ability to juggle a number of different threads of conversation simultaneously led to him being described by Microsoft insiders as 'massively parallel'.[2]

This ability to cope with a multitude of ideas at the same time is reflected in the company's approach. Microsoft is constantly exploring new markets and new software applications. This blanket coverage of the market helps protect the company from missing the significant developments in the industry. And, as Gates was aware, the strategy allowed for the occasional failure.

'We have a multi-product strategy, so while we may have several individual products that have done poorly, when you look at the mix we've done extremely well', said Gates. 'We also have lots of people working on any one question at any one time. To see it working you only have to look at our sales growth; it's almost a straight line going up.'

MULTITASKING MAN

Gates packed more into the average working day than many people manage in a week. During the 30-minute drive from his mansion on Lake Washington to the Microsoft campus in Redmond, for example, he typically spent the entire journey talking on his mobile phone. Often, the conversation continued after he parked, sometimes for over an hour.

The $50 million waterside mansion he had built overlooking Lake Washington in Medina, Washington was also designed to be a multitasking retreat. Along with an underground car park, which houses his collection of sports cars, the mansion has its own beach, sauna and movie theatre. There is also a library that houses among its many volumes, Leonardo da Vinci's Codex Leicester – a work of genius by another famous multitasker. The dining room – described as a pavilion – could seat up to 100 Microsoft employees at any one time.

Part home and part office, the house has been a test bed for all manner of multimedia developments. Like something out of a science fiction movie or a James Bond film, it combines the latest in technology with luxury. For example, it is equipped with state-of-the-art computer entertainment facilities. These include high-definition screens and memory banks linked by fibre optic cables, which enable him to summon up virtually any image in the world. All he has to do is type a subject into his computer keyboard and it appears on the screen.

IMMERSION THERAPY

When he was involved with the day-to-day running of Microsoft one of Gates' toughest challenges was keeping up to date on technological change. With the pressures of running one of the most powerful companies in the world and the proliferation of technologies, trying to keep up to speed is a major problem. Gates is famous for his highly rational approach to problems. It is no surprise therefore to discover that he applied the same kind of approach to managing his own time.

Microsoft is constantly exploring new markets and new software applications. This blanket coverage of the market helps protect the company from missing the significant developments in the industry

In an interview published in *Playboy* magazine, he revealed that he gave up watching television, not because he disliked it but because it was not worthy of an allocation of his time. At his mansion on Lake Washington, Gates keeps a large library with thousands of books – vital for a man whose intellectual curiosity can take him off in any one of a thousand different directions. He stayed abreast of world news, he said, by reading *The Economist* from cover to cover. To ensure his time was used as productively as possible, he always left for the airport at the last minute. This habit led to him reinstating his own parking slot outside Microsoft's Redmond headquarters.

His intellectual discipline even extended to vacations. For a long time he didn't take holidays, believing them to be a sign of weakness. Eventually, however, he relented, but only after finding a way to make them more productive by giving them a theme. On one occasion he went to Brazil and gave the holiday a physics theme. While he was away he read a number of physics books including *The Molecular Biology of the Gene* by James D. Watson.

In order to stay up to speed with new technologies, Gates assembled a collection of the leading experts in a particular technical area and had them provide intensive briefing sessions. The 'think weeks' totally immersed Gates in a subject, during which time he soaked up information like a sponge.

'Even in technology areas it's fun to learn new things', he said. 'When I'm trying to find out where we are going with asynchronous transfer mode, for example, we have experts who come in and talk to me about those things. I spend two weeks here just doing 'think weeks', where I read all the stuff smart people have sent me. I get up to date to see how those pieces fit together.'[3]

OVERDRIVE

With one or two notable exceptions, the speed with which it has managed to get new applications to market has been a characteristic of Microsoft throughout its history, and one that gave Bill Gates an important competitive advantage.

What Gates realized from the start was that getting to market with a good or OK product first is often better than getting there second with a great product. After all, you can always refine the product and eliminate bugs next time round.

Critics of Microsoft were inclined to regard problems with the first version of its software offerings as a major drawback – they still do. But from a strategic point of view, Gates was well aware that it is often more important to get the product out there than it is to get it 100 percent perfect first time.

THE NIMBLE ORGANIZATION

Research tends to support Gates' view. Take, for example, the prize-winning *California Management Review* article by Stanford professor Kathleen Eisenhardt, 'Speed and Strategic Choice: How Managers Accelerate Decision Making'.

The famous article drew on the author's study (with her University of Virginia colleague, Jay Bourgeois) of decision makers in 12 computer firms in Silicon Valley. They found that the slower companies took 12–18 months to achieve what the faster companies managed in just 2–4 months.

In the article, Eisenhardt highlighted five major distinctions between the two groups:

1   The fast decision makers swam in a deep, turbulent sea of real-time information, while the slower ones relied on planning and futuristic information.

2   The fast decision makers tracked a few key operating measures such as bookings, cash and engineering milestones, often updating them daily and scheduling as many as three weekly top management meetings to understand 'what's happening'. They also used a constant email dialogue and face-to-face discussions, rather than the memos and lengthy reports that typified the slow decision makers.

3   The slow decision makers also considered fewer alternatives than their faster counterparts, and minutely dissected each alternative while the greyhounds considered batches of options at the same time.

4   The slowcoaches were 'stymied by conflict', with constant delays; whereas the bullets thrived on conflict, which they saw as a natural and desirable part of the process, but the senior decision maker was also prepared to step in if needed and make a decision. These companies also relied on 'an older and more experienced' mentor for advice, whereas the slow decision makers had no such advisers.

5   Finally, noted Eisenhardt, the fast kids thoroughly integrated strategies and tactics, juggling budgets, schedules, and options simultaneously. The slow kids examined strategy in a vacuum, and were more likely to trip over details on implementing decisions.

SLEEPLESS IN SEATTLE

Gates is famously hyperactive, a characteristic that proved extremely valuable in the computer business. At times it seems he finds it almost impossible to sit still, and his habit of rocking backwards and forwards when he is talking or thinking is well known within the industry. As a businessman, too, Gates was restless, a trait that helped Microsoft avoid the sort of complacency that afflicted rivals such as IBM.

What Gates realized from the start was that getting to market with a good or OK product first is often better than getting there second with a great product

In what is quite probably the fastest-paced industry in the world, it pays to be constantly looking ahead for the next big thing. No matter how successful or rich Gates became, too, he never let up. No doubt it was always a source of great discouragement for his competitors that Gates refused to rest on his laurels. Quite the opposite in fact. There cannot have been many more worrying prospects for his software rivals than the cold and unquestionable certainty that Bill Gates was relentlessly pursuing them with no sign of fatigue.

The fact of the matter is that Gates has one of the most severe cases of intellectual curiosity ever known. When most people kick up and relax on their holiday, Gates was cramming information, consuming book after book just to quench his thirst for new knowledge. It's a characteristic that helps explain the enduring success of Microsoft in an industry where a great many once-successful firms have fallen by the wayside. It is one of the factors that made him such a deadly adversary.

HEDGING HIS BETS

Ever restless, Gates was never content with conquering the US; it became clear that he was looking beyond the shores of America for future opportunities. He invested in the infrastructure of a number of different countries, pumping money into education and university science parks – which many suspected would be a big growth area in the future. Once again, Gates was ahead of the game; hedging his bets on a global scale. It was a strategy borne out of his unique view and synthesis of information.

The Gates view of history in the post-industrial era is instructive. 'Which countries and companies are best prepared to take advantage of the information age that is revolutionizing society? When you think about it, 15 years ago this country [the USA] almost had an inferiority complex about its ability to compete in the world', he said.

'Everybody was talking about how the Japanese had taken over consumer electronics and that the computer industry was going to be next, and that their system of hard work somehow was superior, and that we had to completely rethink what we were doing. Now, if you look at what's happened in personal computers or in business in general, or at how we allocate capital, and how we let labor move around, the US has emerged in a very strong position.

And so the first beneficiary of all this information technology has been the US.'

In his view, Silicon Valley was in the first phase of the revolution, but that didn't guarantee pole position in a later phase. 'In places like Singapore, Hong Kong, and the Scandinavian countries', he noted, 'people are adopting the technology at basically the same rate that we are. And there are a few countries that, relative to their level of income, are going after the technology at an even higher rate than we are because they believe so much in education. In Korea and in many parts of China we see incredible penetration of personal computers even at very low income levels, because people there have decided it's a tool to help their kids get ahead.'

'The whole world is going to benefit in a big way. There will be this shift where, instead of your income level being determined by what country you are from, it will be determined by your education level. Today, a PhD in India doesn't make nearly as much as a PhD in the US. When we get the Internet allowing services and advice to be transported as efficiently as goods are transported via shipping, then you'll get essentially open-market bidding for that engineer in India versus an engineer here in the US. And that benefits everyone, because you're taking better advantage of those resources. So the developed countries will get the early benefit of these things. But in the long run, the people in developing countries who are lucky enough to get a good education should get absolutely the biggest boost from all this.'

> **'In Korea and in many parts of China we see incredible penetration of personal computers even at very low income levels, because people there have decided it's a tool to help their kids get ahead.'**
> **Bill Gates**

COVER ALL THE BASES

A key element of Microsoft's success is its ability to manage a large number of projects simultaneously. Gates is the original multitasking man. When he was working at Microsoft, running the day-to-day business he was said to be able to hold several different technical conversations simultaneously. He also proved to be good at hedging his bets. The secrets of covering all the bases are:

- **Have your finger in lots of pies.** 'We have a multi-product strategy, so while we may have several individual products that have done poorly, when you look at the mix we've done extremely well', said Gates. 'We also have lots of people working on any one question at any one time. To see it working you only have to look at our sales growth; it's almost a straight line going up.'
- **Never stop learning.** In order to stay up to speed with new technologies, Gates assembled a collection of the leading experts in a particular technical area and had them provide intensive briefing sessions. He calls these periods of knowledge cramming 'think weeks' during which time he would soak up information like a sponge.
- **Less haste, more speed.** With one or two notable exceptions, the speed with which it has managed to get new applications to market has been a characteristic of Microsoft throughout its history, and one that gave Bill Gates an important competitive advantage.
- **Stay restless.** Gates is famously hyperactive, a characteristic that proved valuable in the computer business. It was said that he found it almost impossible to sit still and his habit of rocking backwards and forwards when talking or

thinking was well known within the industry. As a business-man, too, Gates was restless, a trait that helped Microsoft avoid the sort of complacency that afflicted rivals such as IBM.

- **Hedge your bets.** Gates looked beyond the US for future business opportunities. He invested in the infrastructure of a number of different countries to spread the risk glo-bally, and pumped money into education. Gates always appeared to be ahead of the game; hedging his bets on a global scale. It was a strategy borne out of his unique view and synthesis of information.

9

BUILD A BYTE-SIZED BUSINESS

'Size works against excellence. Even if we are a big company, we cannot think like a big company or we are dead.'

– Bill Gates

Relative to its stock market valuation, Microsoft has traditionally been a comparatively small company – although it may not seem like it from the outside. Internally, too, the company has constantly split into smaller units to maintain an entrepreneurial environment. At times, change was so rapid that Microsoft seemed to be creating new divisions on an almost weekly basis. Gates also relied on maintaining a simple structure to enable him to keep his grip on the company. Whenever he felt that lines of communication were becoming stretched or fuzzy, he had no hesitation in simplifying the structure.

Gates managed to ingrain the urge to pare down the business into manageable and innovatively sized units into the very ethos of the business. By 2002, Gates was no longer CEO, yet in 2002 Microsoft reorganized into seven financially distinct core business groups. Then not long afterwards in 2005 the company once again reorganized, this time reducing its seven groups to just three divisions:

- Microsoft Platform Products and Services Division – the Windows Client, MSN and Server and Tool groups;

- the Microsoft Business Division – Information Worker and Microsoft Business Solutions groups; and

- Microsoft Entertainment and Devices Division – the Mobile and Embedded Devices and Home and Entertainment groups.

THE SMALLEST BIG COMPANY IN THE WORLD

Although as Microsoft grew it employed many thousands of people around the world, Gates always tried to retain the feel of a small company. 'Even if we are a big company', he said, 'we cannot think like a big company or we are dead. I manage the executive staff. Actually, on paper, there's only a few people who work directly for me. The whole thing is pretty collaborative. We talk about how my time can best be invested; when and how I should assist them to get their jobs done.'

Observers say that Gates was more successful than most computer companies at preserving the initial fun and excitement that made the company a buzzy place to work in the early days. 'We enjoy working together – these are smart people and we have some very hard problems to solve', he said. 'It's a competitive business, and they appreciate all the feedback I give them, including the negative feedback. We are all pretty well paid and we're all having fun – nobody cries too much.'

Each time Microsoft grew too big, Gates split it into smaller units with a maximum of 200 people in each unit. The secret to the structure of Microsoft during Gates time at the helm was that it was geared to the way that its famous CEO works best.

'When we were only 80 people, I knew when everyone came and went. I knew the licence plate number on their cars and their individual projects. I was personally involved with everyone and reviewed every piece of code. Now it's all pretty indirect. We have more than 3000 people in the product development groups alone. Naturally I don't know everyone's names, but I know the key people.'

DIVIDE AND RULE

The way Gates controlled Microsoft is an instructive lesson for anyone grappling with the challenges of managing a large organization. Gates developed his own unique system for controlling Microsoft. He also enjoyed almost unrivalled power for a CEO. In the early 1990s, he reorganized the company to suit his own requirements.

At the top of the organization he placed the office of the president, which consisted of three of his most trusted aides and himself. It acted as the commercial brain of Microsoft.

'Even if we are a big company we cannot think like a big company or we are dead.'

Bill Gates

Beneath this, the company had 15 grades of managers, with about seven people at grade 15. Known as the 'architects', they were the most senior of the company's software developers. Although they were better at writing computer code than Gates, none of them had the collective vision that their famous leader possessed. That fact alone allowed him to dominate them intellectually. Gates has been accused of bullying behaviour in the past, but has insisted that how he treats people depended on what they respond best to as individuals.

Of his top architects he once said: 'Some of them are kind of unusual; you really have to understand them personally. I'm actually friends with all my architects. When I work with the architects there is enough mutual respect that, should we disagree, I make the final decision and we move on.'

This structure means that Gates only had to speak to one group of three and one group of seven people to control the company. It was his own version of divide and rule, and it seemed to work.

LARGE TEAMS THAT WORK LIKE SMALL TEAMS

Early in Microsoft's evolution, Gates came to the conclusion that the best software was created by small groups of developers. When the company decided to move from Seattle, its Redmond Campus was deliberately designed to reinforce a small-group identity. To create the right environment, accommodation was provided in a series of two-storey buildings which allowed team members to interact with their development groups on a daily basis, rather than opt for the classic corporate HQ.

Gates also instituted systems that reinforced the effectiveness of the small team mentality. According to Professor Michael Cusumano at the Massachusetts Institute of Technology (MIT), in Microsoft Bill Gates created a special culture that fostered creativity, both individually and in teams, at the same time as meeting commercial deadlines and demands.[1]

The Microsoft product development philosophy, labelled 'synch-and-stabilize', involved focusing creativity by evolving features and 'fixing' resources; and doing everything in parallel with 'frequent synchronizations.' Exactly what it means is obscure. But clearly, there is method in the madness.

What was striking about the Microsoft approach, said Professor Cusumano, was that the company was not the freewheeling ideas factory it was often portrayed as. In particular, he pointed out that the seemingly relaxed atmosphere was only one part of the picture.

Pizzas may be delivered directly to desks, but there is also a great deal of control – or discipline – at work. It may appear jolly and collegiate, but it is deadly serious. (Interestingly, Tim Jackson's book on Intel produced similar observations of the chip maker.)

For example, the scope and ambition of each and every project is carefully delineated.

The numbers of people involved and the time they spend on a particular project have always been fairly carefully controlled. Some rules are unbending – bugs have to be immediately repaired – to ensure that work is coordinated.

But, as Michael Cusumano pointed out, this is simply good project management as applicable to software development as to any other business where product development is continuous. People are given responsibility and allowed to determine their own working patterns and schedules – up to a point. The boundaries are very clear and simple. People know where they stand, how the system works and what is expected from them. The system works because the people are smart enough to make it work and are highly motivated at the individual level. Their knowledge and creativity is appreciated and rewarded.

MINING THE ETHER ORE

According to management writer and long-time resident of Silicon Valley, Tom Peters: 'Brain based companies have an ethereal character compared to yesterday's outfits, and that's putting it mildly. Time clocks certainly have no place … Barking orders is out. Curiosity, initiative, and the exercise of the imagination are in.'[2]

No one epitomized the switch to intellectual capital more than Bill Gates and Microsoft. Gates was one of the first to recognize that attracting and retaining the best computer programmers was the only way that Microsoft could remain on top. He has mined the ether ore of his 'high IQ' knowledge workers ever since.

Key to his success was the fact that he was not greedy, and was prepared to share the company's wealth around through stock options. According to one magazine he made more people rich than any other man in history – inside and outside Microsoft.

THE RISE OF THE KNOWLEDGE WORKER

According to the experts, the switch from physical work to intellectual work – 'brawn to brain' – is already well under way in the developed economies. Phrases such as the 'information age' and 'knowledge workers' have been around for some time.

The consensus among the experts is that intellectual capital – made up of knowledge and ideas – is now replacing physical capital – factories and machines – as the key driver of wealth creation. Intellectual assets, then, are now more valuable than those that have traditionally enjoyed pride of place in annual reports.

If intellectual capital is the new competitive imperative, then new ways of managing those assets are required. It is against the background of the new knowledge economy that Bill Gates emerged as a powerful new leadership model.

> **People are given responsibility and allowed to determine their own working patterns and schedules – up to a point. The boundaries are very clear and simple. People know where they stand, how the system works and what is expected from them**

Many of the world's biggest companies fell over themselves to jump on the knowledge bandwagon, and embrace the latest panacea for business success. Such was the corporate enthusiasm for know-how that several companies created the job of chief knowledge officer. Xerox Corporation, General Electric, and Hewlett-Packard were just some of the serious-minded companies that attempted to corral ideas and know-how. For Bill Gates there was far less reason to take action on the knowledge front; he had already been successfully capturing and utilizing knowledge at Microsoft for over two decades.

UNLEASHING THE MICRO-SERFS

The way the company was organized also encouraged entrepreneurial activity among Microsoft employees, and acted as a failsafe on Gates himself. So, for example, Jeff Lill was part of the development team responsible for building an on-line service to compete with AOL (America Online), Prodigy and CompuServe, the market leaders at that time. The team felt that the Internet did not have sufficient priority within Microsoft, which had been slow in developing a response to the information 'superhighway'.

When the project was presented to Gates, he was highly sceptical that they would be able to complete it on time. Despite his reservations, however, Gates gave it the 'green light' and authorized additional resources so they could try. The team then took themselves off to an isolated part of the Microsoft campus. They declared the area the 'Microsoft Enterprise Zone' and worked on developing the application in isolation from the rest of the company.

As Lill explained: 'It was perfect. It was off by itself. Nobody was going to bug us ... I called it the Microsoft Enterprise Zone because it was this little crappy place, but great because we had the room we needed; and frankly, I liked being away from the rest of the campus. I wanted to avoid a big political situation, where everybody wanted a finger in our pie and needed to know our plans. I really wanted to be way out there on the side so we could get this done and get it launched.'[3]

Mobility is also important. Developers move from one project to another, jockeying for a place on the most exciting new start-ups. It has been an important part of the Microsoft culture for individuals to earn their spurs in this way. For Microsoft veterans, successful product releases are like campaign medals, to be displayed with pride. Reputations are based on track record and technical skills.

Status symbols have always been conspicuously absent at Microsoft. Virtually all offices at the Redmond campus were designed with similar furniture and dimensions – nine feet by twelve feet. This reinforced the egalitarian culture, eliminating potential squabbles about office size, but it also had another more practical purpose. Standardizing the office size made internal moves much easier to execute. This is an important point in a company where reorganizations are common. The design meant that the facilities management staff at Microsoft could, if necessary, move 200 people into different offices overnight.

Intellectual assets, then, are now more valuable than those that have traditionally enjoyed pride of place in annual reports

Only senior managers received bigger offices: two nine-by-twelve offices from which the separating wall has been removed. Gates, even when a full-time employee, had a modest office, and refused to accept a designated parking space for many years until he realized that without it he could not expect to leave for the airport at the very last minute and still hope to catch his plane.

BUILD A BYTE-SIZED BUSINESS

Relative to its stock market valuation, Microsoft has always been a comparatively small company. Internally, too, the company has constantly split into smaller units to maintain an entrepreneurial environment. At times, change was so rapid that Microsoft seemed to be creating new divisions on an almost weekly basis. Gates also relied on maintaining a simple structure to enable him to keep his grip on the company.

- **Create a small team culture.** Early in Microsoft's evolution, Gates came to the conclusion that the best software was created by small groups of developers. When the company decided to move from Seattle, its Redmond Campus was deliberately designed to reinforce a small-group identity.
- **Keep the feel of a small company.** Although Microsoft employed many thousands of people around the world, Gates tried to retain the feel of a small company. 'Even if we are a big company', Gates said, 'we cannot think like a big company or we are dead'.
- **Keep reporting lines short.** Gates developed his own unique system for controlling Microsoft. In the early 1990s, he reorganized the company to suit his own requirements. He only had to stay in contact with a small number of managers to control the company.
- **Share your wealth around.** Through stock options, Gates probably made more people rich than any other man in history. This is a great motivator.
- **Create a meritocracy.** There were virtually no status symbols at Microsoft. Respect had to be earned.

10

NEVER, EVER, TAKE YOUR EYE OFF THE BALL

'Products are always gonna be obsolete so you'd better enjoy doing the next version. It's like pinball – if you play a good game, the reward is that you get to play another one.'

– Bill Gates[1]

Gates was at the top of the tech world for more than three decades. Early on at Microsoft he became the richest man in the world – not bad for someone who was still in his 30s – even now he has only just passed the 50 mark. Yet despite his enormous wealth and achievements, Gates showed little sign of slowing down. He said he was driven by a 'latent fear' that he might miss the next big thing. He had no intention of repeating the mistakes of other dominant computer companies such as IBM and Apple. 'I know very well that in the next ten years, if Microsoft is still a leader, we will have had to weather at least three crises', he says.[2]

THE THOUGHTS OF CHAIRMAN BILL

In the 1990s, Gates felt the need to share his vision with the rest of us. His book *The Road Ahead*, which set out his view of the technological future, was quickly followed by *Business @ the Speed of Thought*. The sudden rush to commit his thoughts to paper prompted some to wonder whether Gates' vanity was starting to get the better of him. Although the books generated a huge amount of interest, their message was not as inspiring or exciting as some had hoped.

Some commentators saw great irony, too, in his choice of the traditional paper book format to communicate his vision of the future. The subject matter of his books encompassed the obsolescence of pre-electronic media, yet was delivered by a medium that would have been familiar to William Caxton in the fifteenth century. Although published in multimedia format, in the case of *The Road Ahead* at least, readers reported that the original CD-ROM version was full of technical glitches – giving new resonance to the phrase 'the medium is the message'.

To be fair, Gates admitted he was wrong as often as everyone else in the computer industry. His argument was that he could afford to be wrong more often because he had so many projects on the go at any one time. 'I synthesize a lot of information to get a broad picture', he explained. 'So there are cases where I'll decide things a bit differently. But I'm the CEO and the technical strategy is in my hands. Sometimes I'm completely alone in my opinions if it's a technical question or a strategy problem.

Some commentators saw great irony, too, in his choice of the traditional paper book format to communicate his vision of the future

'When it comes to a product decision there have been many cases when I analyse things in my own unique way. However if it is a business-type decision, rarely is my conviction sufficient to go it alone. Usually I'd take the time to get people to explain their views more clearly. That's my job and what's the point of having me here if I can't make my mind up.'

DON'T LOOK BACK

'I have often thought that if Microsoft were a car, we'd have a very large gas pedal and a very small brake. There'd be a very large windscreen at the front to see where we were going, but no rear-view mirror – we know the competition is right on our tail, so we don't need to look back', said Mike Murray, the former vice president of Human Resources at Microsoft.[3]

Fundamental to Microsoft's success was Gates' willingness to keep his eyes firmly on the road ahead. 'Looking in the rear-view mirror is

… a waste of time, basically', Gates has said. The comment is reminiscent of Henry Ford, who said: 'history is more or less bunk'.

But Gates was always well aware of the context in which he was operating. He had a keen sense, too, of the history of both his industry and the march of technology through the centuries. According to Randall E. Stross, author of *The Microsoft Way,* Gates was being disingenuous when he said that he never looks in the rear-view mirror.

'He has looked back all the time – frequently, insistently, systematically', says Stross. 'He cites historical examples whenever he discusses future strategy. He uses an historical perspective when he notes that in the commercial history of computing, no company that was the leader in one era succeeded in maintaining its position in the next one, and when he worries that Microsoft's place in the personal computer era may "disqualify" it from maintaining its place in the coming network-centred era. Gates' historical sensibility saturates his analysis of the present and the future, but he simply does not label it as such.'

INTO THE SUNSET?

With his remarkable track record over the past two decades it was inevitable that people would ask what happens to Microsoft without Bill Gates. Although he successfully handed the CEO baton to Steve Ballmer, we will see how he managed a spectacularly successful transition out of the business. Gates continued to cast a huge shadow in Redmond and the IT industry in general in the early days after his move to Chief Software Architect.

Regardless of the switch in job title, initially Gates remained Microsoft's natural leader. Towards the end of 2001, for example, at the launch of the new Microsoft operating system Windows XP, Gates was still very much to the fore amid the razzamatazz. The lavish marketing initiative was said to have cost in the region of $500 million worldwide.

In New York City, Microsoft paraded its patriotic colours. A gospel choir sang America the Beautiful, before Gates, flanked by NYC Mayor Rudy Giuliani, took the stage and pledged his support for the global fight against terrorism and even seemed to suggest that the advent of Microsoft's new OS would help revive the flagging IT industry. Gates was not only making a transition out of Microsoft it seemed, but in a more personal way was transforming from the awkward, sometimes inarticulate computer nerd to become an accomplished showman in his own right.

Gates was set to stick around for some time ... But he was already mentally preparing himself and the shareholders for the next step

Gates was set to stick around for some time. He was still there in 2007 launching the Vista OS, his last big OS launch. But he was already mentally preparing himself and the shareholders for the next step. The transfer of power from one leader to the next can have a major impact, not just on morale and business performance but on the company's share price. The concern was that without Gates Microsoft would lose its mojo. Gates' response was this: 'The whole notion in the press of personifying a company through one person or a few people is a gross simplification, and it totally misstates the picture.'[4]

THE DIGITAL SAGE

For obvious reasons, right up until his departure from Microsoft on a full-time basis, and possibly even beyond, Gates generates a certain amount of awe among those who regard him as the predictor and architect of the digital age. To be fair, some, if not all, of his reputation as a visionary is deserved. History may judge him more kindly than his many detractors and rivals who argued that he was simply exploiting his monopoly position. Without Gates and Microsoft, it is unlikely whether the PC revolution would be as advanced as it is. Yet Gates was much too smart to rest on his laurels. More than any other figure in his industry he understood just what a treacherous road he was driving along. After all, he saw the cars in front drive over the cliff more than once.

> **'The technology business has a lot of twists and turns … Probably the reason it's such a fun business is that no company gets to rest on its laurels.'**
> **Bill Gates**

'The technology business has a lot of twists and turns', he noted. 'Probably the reason it's such a fun business is that no company gets to rest on its laurels. IBM was more dominant than any company will ever be in technology, and yet they missed a few turns in the road. That makes you wake up every day thinking, "Hmm, let's try to make sure today's not the day we miss the turn in the road. Let's find out what's going on in speech recognition, or in artificial intelligence. Let's make sure we're hiring the kinds of people who can pull those things together, and let's make sure we don't get surprised."

'Sometimes we do get taken by surprise. For example, when the Internet came along, we had it as a fifth or sixth priority. It wasn't like somebody told me about it and I said, "I don't know how to spell that." I said, "Yeah, I've got that on my list, so I'm okay." But there came a point when we realized it was happening faster and was a much deeper phenomenon than had been recognized in our strategy. So as an act of leadership I had to create a sense of crisis, and we spent a couple of months throwing ideas and email around, and we went on some retreats. Eventually a new strategy coalesced, and we said, "Okay, here's what we're going to do; here's how we're going to measure ourselves internally; and here's what the world should think about what we're going to do."

'That kind of crisis is going to come up every three or four years. You have to listen carefully to all the smart people in the company. That's why a company like ours has to attract a lot of people who think in different ways, it has to allow a lot of dissent, and then it has to recognize the right ideas and put some real energy behind them.'

THE QUICK AND THE DEAD

Whatever the limitations of his vision, Gates has been the closest thing the computer industry has to Leonardo Da Vinci, the famous Renaissance futurist whose drawings of fantastical machines became a reality centuries later.

Apart from his collection of sports cars and a multimillion dollar mansion on the outskirts of Seattle, Gates is surprisingly restrained in his spending. But there is of course that glorious exception, his purchase of the Leicester Codex by Leonardo Da Vinci for $30.8 million. There are those that have suggested Gates sees himself as a latter-day Da Vinci – someone whose visions of the future are proved accurate in following centuries.

Unlike his hero, however, Gates is rooted in the here and now, whether solving Microsoft software problems, or tackling global hunger. One of his greatest attributes is his ability to combine technological innovation with a hard-nosed pragmatism. He also recognizes his own limitations – an unusual trait in such an accomplished individual.

'You have to be careful, if you're good at something, to make sure you don't think you're good at other things that you aren't necessarily so good at', he has noted. 'I come in every day and work with a great team of people who are trying to figure out how to make great software, listening to the feedback and doing the research. And it's very typical that because I've been very successful at that, people come in and expect that I have wisdom about topics that I don't.

'I do think there are some ways that we've run the company – the way we've hired people, and created an environment and used stock options – that would be good lessons for other businesses as well. But I always want to be careful not to suggest that we've found the solutions to all problems.'[6]

Ultimately, though, it was Bill Gates' restlessness that more than any other factor explains Microsoft's success and will no doubt drive his philanthropic foundation forward to greater achievements.

He always understood that the rapidity of change in his industry was fundamental to the competitive position of the company he created. Microsoft was faster on its feet than the rest of the pack. But to maintain its position, its famous leader was never afraid to abandon the past to pursue the future. Gates more than any other figure of the twenty-first century understood what the phrase 'technological revolution' really meant. He knew there were only the quick and the dead.

NEVER, EVER, TAKE YOUR EYE OFF THE BALL

Gates was at the top of his profession for more than three decades. In that time he became the richest man in the world. Yet despite his enormous wealth and achievements, Gates showed no signs of slowing down. If you want to do business at the speed of Gates:

- **Don't try to explain.** Gates has felt the need to share his vision with the rest of us. After *The Road Ahead,* for example, which set out his view of the technological future, some wondered whether Gates' vanity was starting to get the better of him.
- **Don't look back.** Fundamental to Microsoft's success was Gates' willingness to keep his eyes firmly on the road ahead. 'Looking in the rear-view mirror is … a waste of time, basically', Gates said. Yet he was well aware of his historical context.
- **Create the future.** Gates generated a certain amount of awe among those who regarded him as the predictor and architect of the digital age. History may judge him more kindly than his many detractors and rivals who argued that he was simply exploiting his monopoly position.
- **Stay hungry.** Microsoft was faster on its feet than the rest of the pack. To maintain its position, its famous leader was never afraid to abandon the past to pursue the future. Gates knew that, in the tech industry at least, there were only the quick and the dead.

KNOW WHEN IT'S TIME TO MOVE ON

'I've done the same thing for 33 years, in a sense … It will be an adjustment for me. If I didn't have the Foundation – which is so exciting, and the work is complex – if I didn't have that, it would be tough for me, because I'm not a sit-on-the-beach type.'

– Bill Gates

Managing a CEO succession is not easy. You've got to know when it's time to go, help find someone to be your replacement, manage the transition, and then move on and find something else to do. No wonder that so many CEO successions fail.

Great business leaders like Gates know when it is time to step up to the plate and take charge, and when it's time to delegate. And, just as importantly, the best leaders know when it is time to take a step back. But knowing that the time is approaching to hand over the reins, and actually seeing it through are two different things. Many great CEOs find it difficult to hand over power. They don't always select the right people to step in. They find it hard to let go.

Business history is littered with difficult CEO successions at high profile companies. While Gates was contemplating his future at Microsoft in the late 1990s, Robert Nakasone became CEO of Toys R Us in 1998 but left just 18 months later, Richard Thoman sat in the hot seat at Xerox for barely a year, taking the job in April 1999 and departing in May 2000.

Like almost everything else Gates has been involved with, however, once he had taken the decision to move on, and applied his substantial intellect to the challenge of succession, he came up with a remarkably effective solution.

SECRETS OF SUCCESSION

Business academics have agonized over CEO succession for years, devoting considerable research and many articles to the subject. It is no surprise when you consider how difficult even the most celebrated CEOs have found the process.

At General Electric, for example, Jack Welch was feted as one of the leading chief executives of his generation, yet when it came to organizing his succession Welch seemed reluctant to step down. Welch's decision to retire from GE as CEO in April 2001 was announced in advance, meticulous planning meant that three potential leadership candidates were nurtured, everything was in place, ready. In October, just six months before his retirement, the succession was put on hold until the end of 2001. Welch announced his successor Jeff Immelt in November 2000 prompting the departure of the other two candidates, with Welch eventually stepping down in September 2001.

Like almost everything else Gates has been involved with ... once he had taken the decision to move on, and applied his substantial intellect to the challenge of succession, he soon came up with a remarkably effective solution

Perhaps more relevant is the succession story of Gates' arch-rival Steve Jobs. John Sculley was appointed from Pepsi in 1983, then usurped Apple CEO and co-founder Jobs, with Jobs leaving in 1985. Sculley was pushed out in 1993, and his replacement Michael Spindler lasted until 1996. The next CEO, Gil Amelio, brought Jobs back in but was himself deposed in 1997, leaving Jobs in charge again. Confused? The shareholders were by the way the stock price bombed. Fortunately for Apple and the shareholders, Jobs remains at the helm. Let's hope Jobs is able to implement a managed succession when he finally decides to step down.

Warren Bennis is a business professor at the University of Southern California and has written extensively about succession. His view is that problems stem from the way that boards go about appointing successors. 'Boards that go into rhapsodic overtures about leadership never really define what they mean by that word, nor do they pay enough attention to the human factors', he says.

In their *Harvard Business Review* article 'Don't Hire the Wrong CEO' Bennis and James O'Toole, Professor of Business Ethics at the Daniels College of Business, Denver University, identify seven areas boards need to get right:

- Arrive at a shared definition of leadership.

- Resolve strategic and political conflicts.

- Look for and assess the soft qualities in CEO candidates.

- Don't be seduced by charisma; just because someone acts like a CEO doesn't mean that they would make a good CEO.

- The best leaders are not usually the safe choice.

- Assess internal candidates with the same rigour as external ones.

- Don't rush the decision.

PEOPLE POWER

For the founders of companies, letting go must be doubly difficult. How hard it must be to hand over a business that you have created or co-created, and then entrust the future of that business to others. Some entrepreneurs are comparatively quick to hand over responsibility for day-to-day running, usually because they believe that other people can add more value in the CEO role, or bring something different to the table.

Gates though has proved a rare combination of entrepreneur, technical wizard, brilliant strategist and business leader. He was as formidable a CEO as he was software architect. Effective succession is partly, although not entirely, about getting the right person – or people – to take over. With Microsoft the task was complicated by the fact that Gates assumed multiple roles at the company. He was the software developer and code warrior, hands-on business manager and CEO visionary, the company cheerleader, and the external face and voice of the corporation.

> **'Boards that go into rhapsodic overtures about leadership never really define what they mean by that word, nor do they pay enough attention to the human factors'**
> **Warren Bennis**

In the end Gates engineered his replacement – if it is possible to replace as formidable a talent as Gates – by appointing not one but several Microsoft executives to cover his various roles. One of the first to be selected as part of the Gates succession was Steve Ballmer. A long time friend of the Microsoft co-founder, they met back in Gates' college days as Harvard University classmates. Recruited by Gates in 1980 in the early Microsoft era, Ballmer was moved into the CEO role in 2000, but with Gates still at the company his role was always likely to be overshadowed until the founder's departure.

An extrovert, Ballmer has orchestrated the marketing side, and is well known for his loud and forceful presentations. In many ways Ballmer has been the yin to Gates' yang. Indeed Gates once described Ballmer as his opposite in a *Computer Reseller News* article. Unsurprisingly Gates and Ballmer have clashed many times as Microsoft has grown over the years, but they learnt to find a way of working together that first and foremost benefited the company that they were both passionate about.

Lined up alongside Ballmer was Ray Ozzie, who adopted the chief software architect role putting him in charge of technical strategy and product development. No slouch in the software smarts department, Ozzie created the Lotus Notes software, arriving at Microsoft courtesy of one of the company's famous IQ plus promising software raids, when it acquired Ozzie's firm Groove Networks in 2005. Ozzie was working in collaborative software at Groove Networks – it became Microsoft Office Groove. It is worth noting that Gates chose a person interested in mechanisms for collaboration, in an Internet age dominated by so-called social media.

Gates made sure that he went graciously, in good humour, and with the right vision-affirming, employee-rallying, parting message

For the visionary role Gates picked Craig Mundie, who was designated chief research and strategy officer. Hired in 1992, Mundie was originally brought in to work on non-PC computing at Microsoft. His field of expertise was supercomputers, with Gates anticipating the increasingly availability and importance of super computing power in our everyday lives.

And then there are the technical fellows, a small group of people about 20 or so strong. These people are responsible for many of the technical innovations produced by Microsoft, the employees that Gates often described as the real experts.

GRACIOUS GOODBYES

Once you have made the decision to go it is important to say goodbye on the right note. Gates made sure that he went graciously, in good humour, and with the right vision-affirming, employee-rallying, parting message. He had plenty of opportunities to reinforce his transition message, at a news conference at the Redmond HQ on 15 June, 2006, at his final Consumer Electronics Show keynote speech in January 2008 and, in particular, on his last day of work as full-time employee at Microsoft on Friday, 27 June 2008. Each time, Gates acquitted himself well, with assured, heartfelt, sometimes amusing, even touching performances.

While harbouring a reputation as a hard taskmaster when it came to making sure he got intellectual added value out of others, Gates had no problem acknowledging the essential contribution that Microsoft employees made to the success of the organization. When announcing his two year transition plan in June 2006, for example, Gates said: 'I have one of the best jobs in the world. I love software, and I love working with the smart, creative, passionate people at Microsoft. Together, we've built a great company whose products have empowered people around the world.'[1]

Belying his image as a hard nosed, no-holds-barred business leader, Gates showed an endearing ability to be wryly self-deprecating in the run up to his transition from Microsoft to his Foundation. At 6.40pm on a Sunday evening in January 2008, Gates stepped out in front of 5000 or so people at the Venetian Hotel's Palazzo Ballroom in Las Vegas to give his last keynote speech at the Consumer Electronics Show.

He hadn't been on the stage for long before surmising what his last day at work later that June would be like and then introducing a short film clip that envisaged that day.[2] In the film Gates pokes fun at himself with the aid of various celebrities. Gates is seen struggling to master an exercise ball in the gym under the tutelage of actor Matthew McConaughey; interrupting U2's Bono, pre-gig, in an attempt to persuade him to displace U2 guitarist, The Edge, on the strength of Gates' Guitar Hero performance; demonstrating a

Hollywood show reel, suggesting a career in politics to Hillary Clinton; and bizarrely rapping 'Big pimpin' I'm Bill G! Big pimpin' yeah you know me', to Jay-Z in a music studio.

It is a side of Bill G that not many people will have seen outside of his personal friends and Microsoft, but it was a great exercise as part of building a legacy beyond the concept of Bill the Ruthless. It was also consistent with the increased post-Warren Buffett friendship emphasis on Gates having fun doing whatever it is that he does.

NEW PRODUCTS, NEW DIRECTIONS

The world has changed dramatically over the last two decades, in particular with the rapid transformation in information and communications technology. The rise in importance of the Internet and the convergence of technology onto small portable devices like mobile phones and MP3 players created significant challenges for Microsoft, possibly challenges that Gates was not best placed to meet.

While Gates moved to Chief Software Architect, CEO Ballmer pressed ahead with a range of diverse products. These included a video games platform the Xbox, competing with Nintendo and Sony, Internet Protocol television (IPTV), the Zune music player, the Bing search engine, and Windows Mobile, a smart-phone software platform. A diverse set of products these might be, but they have yet to make the kind of impact or achieve the kind of dominance that Microsoft is accustomed to with its products.

And, while it was part of Gates' job, as he acknowledges, to send some tough talking emails critiquing Microsoft product development, a famous email sent in 2003 reveals Gates' deep seated frustration at the usability of a particular Microsoft product.[3]

Beginning 'I am quite disappointed at how Windows Usability has been going backwards', Gates proceeds to rant: about the Microsoft.com website – 'this site is so slow it is unusable'; about the website search and downloading –'it is more like a puzzle that you get to solve'; Windows Update – 'where I get to see weird dialog boxes'; about the install – 'Amazing how slow this thing is'; and it gets worse.

The rise in importance of the Internet and the convergence of technology onto small portable devices ... created significant challenges for Microsoft, possibly challenges that Gates was not best placed to meet

Asked about the email Gates replied, 'There's not a day that I don't send a piece of email … like that piece of email. That's my job.' He even referred to it in his farewell address.

As organizations grow their founders often become less able to influence what happens within them. In a way Microsoft had outgrown Gates, both in terms of what he was able to contribute to the company by way of technical knowledge and influence appropriate for succeeding in the modern market, and also what Microsoft was able to offer him in terms of the kind of challenge that he needed to push his intellect and abilities to the maximum, and keep him satisfied on a personal level. When that happens it is usually time to move on.

GATES THE PHILANTHROPIST

It is not a good idea to step down from a full time job without knowing what you are going to do next. Gates had a pretty good idea of what lay ahead when he finished full-time at Microsoft.

To start with there was a holiday: 'I've never taken more than a two-week vacation, and this time it will actually be about seven weeks, so that is very long.' Although in true Gates fashion it wasn't all holiday. It also included some Microsoft work.

Then there are the investments. Gates is best known for co-founding Microsoft, but he also founded Corbis, a very successful digital art and photography archive. He has money invested in a project being organized by former Microsoft Chief Technology Officer Nathan Myhrvold, working on a new type of nuclear reactor. And there are other investments too. Plus there will be continued involvement in the occasional project at Microsoft where Gates remains chairman for the foreseeable future and plans to spend one day a week.

And there are the hobbies. Gates, along with Buffett, is a keen bridge player. The pair even offered $1 million to encourage high schools to promote bridge to school children.

Most of Gates time, however, will be devoted to his new challenge and longstanding passion, the Bill & Melinda Gates Foundation which dates back to 1994. Gates is following in the philanthropic footsteps of American tycoons such as Henry Ford, John D. Rockefeller, and Andrew Carnegie, who all devoted large sums of money to charitable foundations in their later years.

The Foundation employs nearly 800 people, has an endowment of $34.17 billion, and has committed total grants of $21.08 billion in the US and across the world. Buffett has also pledged to donate a significant proportion of his wealth, in effect doubling the Foundation's resources.

The focus is on global heath and development, as well as a US programme that focuses on education, health and other issues. 'I believe that with great wealth comes great responsibility, a responsibility to give back to society, a responsibility to see that those resources are put to work in the best possible way to help those most in need', said Gates in an interview with the *Seattle Post-Intelligencer*.[4] 'Many years ago, I made it clear that almost all of my wealth would be returned to society through a Foundation.'

He is also bringing the same strategies to the world of philanthropy that made Microsoft so successful: 'assembling a team of very bright people, optimistic people, providing them the resources they need, encouraging them to think big and come up with long-term solutions'.

Gates is relishing the challenge, and believes that it has the 'three magical elements' that led him to enjoy his time at Microsoft so much. 'First there are opportunities for big breakthroughs … Second, I feel like my experience in building teams of smart people with different skill sets focused on tough long-term problems can be a real contribution … Finally, I find the intelligence and dedication of the people involved in these issues to be just as impressive as what I have seen before … The opportunity to gather smart, creative people into teams and give them resources and guidance as they tackle the challenges is very fulfilling', he says.

LOGGING OFF

With luck, Gates will be as successful with the work of the Foundation as he was at Microsoft. For many of us however, Gates will always be the brilliant geek that founded Microsoft, that helped to popularize the PC, and that brought the Windows OS to billions of computer users across the world.

Judging by his farewell comments to Microsoft employees on his last day at work, Gates feels much the same way. As he left, he logged off with these words: 'There won't be a day of my life that I'm not thinking about Microsoft and the great things that it's doing, and wanting to help. So thank you for making it the center of my life, and so much fun.'

KNOW WHEN IT'S TIME TO MOVE ON

Great CEOs know when it is time to move on to new challenges. The way Gates has managed his exit from Microsoft should be lesson to all leaders:

- **Great timing.** Be your own critic. If you feel that others can offer more value than you are able to, or you are no longer motivated by the challenge, it is time to move on.
- **Exit gradually.** First Gates worked alongside the new CEO, and then appointed people to cover the numerous roles he has acquired over the years.
- **Exit graciously.** Gates was both quick to praise the people who had contributed to his success, and good humoured in making his transition. It generates a lot of goodwill.
- **Find new challenges.** Gates didn't retire. He moved on to new challenges. In his work with the Bill & Melissa Gates Foundation, however, he will continue to use those characteristics and strategies that served him so well while he was creating the biggest and most successful software company in the world.

HOW TO GET RICH THE
BILL GATES WAY

Heading up the *Fortune* magazine 2009 billionaires list for yet another year, Bill Gates is the richest man on the planet. The title of most valuable US Corporation in the world is a hotly contested one, the companies change frequently depending on the fortunes of different industry sectors, but there is no question that Gates presaged the beginning of a new technological age when the value of Microsoft surpassed that of GE in 1998. Spectacularly successful for over three decades, and despite his departure to help out at the Bill & Melinda Gates Foundation, Bill Gates can justifiably lay claim to the title of the King of the Nerds. (Asked by the American journalist Connie Chung if he regarded himself as a nerd, Gates replied: 'If nerd means you can enjoy understanding the insides of a computer and sit in front of it for hours and play with it and enjoy it.' What he didn't say, but could have, is that his nerdish hobbies made him the richest man in the world.)

How did Gates achieve so much in such a comparatively short space of time, and then against intense competition, maintain his company's dominance in its market over several decades?

A careful analysis of the way Bill Gates ran Microsoft points to eleven secrets of his success. For those who want to follow in his footsteps, here they are.

1   Be in the right place at the right time

In the era of the knowledge worker, technical know-how and creativity are the new corporate assets. The ability to combine these attributes with business acumen and a highly competitive streak, makes Bill Gates one of a very rare breed of entrepreneurs. But we must not forget that luck played its part too; a remarkable piece of good fortune carried him to an altitude where his special talents could flourish.

2 Fall in love with the technology

Bill Gates has had a lifelong love affair with the personal computer. From the very beginning, Gates and his partner Paul Allen could see that the PC would change everything. The two would talk late into the night about what the post-PC world would be like. They never truly doubted that the revolution would come. 'It's going to happen' was an article of faith for the fledgling Microsoft, and they were going to write software for it when it did.

3 Take no prisoners

Gates was a fierce competitor. In everything he does, he has been driven to win. This made him an extremely tough adversary. He made no bones about this and talked openly about crushing the competition.

4 Hire very smart people

Gates has consistently sought out and hired the smartest individuals both at Microsoft, and at the Bill & Melinda Gates Foundation. This deliberate strategy has ensured that Microsoft attracts the highest calibre staff in its industry. Some people accused Gates of being elitist, but he was one of the first entrepreneurs to truly understand what intellectual capital is all about.

5   Learn to survive

In Microsoft, Bill Gates created a voracious learning machine. It was, he believed, the sign of a 'smart organization', and the only way to avoid making the same mistake twice. His competitors were not so careful. By capitalizing on the mistakes of others, Microsoft prospered.

6   Don't expect any thanks

If there is one lesson that Bill Gates learnt the hard way it is that fame and infamy are never far apart. You can't expect to become the richest man in the world without making some enemies – and in the computer industry, Gates had more than his share.

7   Assume the visionary position

Bill Gates was one of the first of a new type of business leader. Over the years, he repeatedly demonstrated that he was the closest thing the computer industry had to a seer. His in-depth understanding of technology and unique way of synthesizing data gave him a special ability to spot future trends and steer Microsoft's strategy. This also inspired awe among Microsoft fans and intimidated competitors.

8   Cover all the bases

A key element of Microsoft's success is its ability to manage a large number of projects simultaneously. Gates himself is the original multitasking man, and is said to be able to hold several different technical conversations simultaneously. He has also shown himself to be a master of hedging his bets.

9 Build a byte-sized business

Relative to its stock market valuation, Microsoft remains a comparatively small company. Internally, too, the company has constantly split into smaller units to maintain an entrepreneurial environment. At times, change was so rapid that Microsoft seemed to be creating new divisions on an almost weekly basis. Gates also relied on maintaining a simple structure to enable him to keep his grip on the company.

10 Never, ever, take your eye off the ball

Gates was at the top of his profession for more than three decades. In that time he has become the richest man in the world. Yet, despite his enormous wealth and achievements, Gates continued to work very long hours at Microsoft.

And finally ... know when it's time to move on.

Great CEOs know when it is time to move on to new challenges. The way Gates managed his exit from Microsoft should be a lesson to all leaders. Gates transitioned out of his full time role at Microsoft gradually and graciously: shifting seamlessly to the fresh philanthropic challenge of helping to run the Bill & Melinda Gates Foundation.

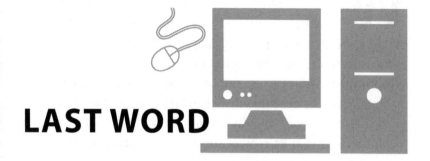

LAST WORD

What are we to make of Bill Gates rise to prominence? As Randall E. Stross, author of *The Microsoft Way*, puts it: 'Essentially, we have two choices. On the one hand, we can accept a characterization of Gates as the Antichrist, Microsoft as the evil empire, its software as junk, and the company's success as rooted in deceptions, outright lies, legal trickery, and brute-force marketing. On the other hand, we can take the company at its own word that it has benevolently ushered in the personal computer revolution and that its market success is the just reward for the service it has rendered the public.'[1]

There are two sides to any story. Stross's own research, which included access to the Microsoft archives, led him to favour the latter explanation. But whatever your views on his business practices, Gates cannot be ignored. In the history of business there has never been an entrepreneur so successful so young. Nor has there ever been anyone who made so many other people so rich so quickly.

Computer visionary or ruthless monopolist? Messiah or Antichrist? Bill Gates provokes extreme reactions, of that there is no doubt. In the end, however, the reality is probably less fantastic. He is a very smart man, of immense energy and driven to win. But there is something of the Wizard of Oz about Gates. For all his undoubted intellect he cannot possibly live up to the size of the image he projects to the outside world.

For all the hype and all the accusations, one thing about Gates shines through: he became the greatest of all the computer entrepreneurs because he had both the technical smarts to understand what's just around the corner, and the commercial smarts to sell it to the rest of us. This combination of talents makes Bill Gates one of a very rare breed of entrepreneurs.

Gates was there standing on the threshold of the PC revolution, to usher in the new era. For this reason alone, there will never be another quite like him.

NOTES

THE LIFE AND TIMES OF BILL GATES

1   *Forbes*, September 1998
2   Wallace, James and Erickson, Jim, *Hard Drive: Bill Gates and the Making of the Microsoft Empire*, John Wiley, New York, 1992
3   Wallace, James and Erickson, Jim, *Hard Drive: Bill Gates and the Making of the Microsoft Empire*, John Wiley, New York, 1992
4   Wallace, James and Erickson, Jim, *Hard Drive: Bill Gates and the Making of the Microsoft Empire*, John Wiley, New York, 1992

CHAPTER 1

1   Stross, Randall E., *The Microsoft Way*, Addison-Wesley, 1996

CHAPTER 2

1   Schlender, Brent, 'Bill Gates and Paul Allen talk', *Fortune*, October 2, 1995
2   Stross, Randall E., *The Microsoft Way*, Addison-Wesley, 1996
3   Peters, Thomas, *Liberation Management*, Alfred A. Knopf Inc., 1992
4   Roos, Johan, 'Intellectual Capital: what you can measure you can manage', *Perspectives for Managers*, Vol 26, No. 10, IMD, November 1996
5   Schendler, Brent, 'The Bill and Warren show', *Fortune*, July 20, 1998

CHAPTER 3

1   Kehoe, Louise and Dixon, Hugo, 'Fightback at the seat of power', *Financial Times*, June 10, 1996

2   'Watching his Windows', Forbes ASAP, 1997, taken from Jager, Rama D. and Ortiz, Rafael, *In the Company of Giants*, McGraw-Hill, New York, 1997

CHAPTER 4

1   Stross, Randall E., *The Microsoft Way*, Addison-Wesley, New York, 1996
2   Morris, Betsy, 'The Wealth Builders', *Fortune*, December 11, 1995
3   Schlender, Brent, 'The Bill and Warren Show', *Fortune*, July 20, 1998
4   Stross, Randall E., *The Microsoft Way*, Addison-Wesley, New York, 1996
5   Jager, Rama D. and Ortiz, Rafael, *In the Company of Giants*, McGraw-Hill, New York, 1997
6   Jager, Rama D. and Ortiz, Rafael, *In the Company of Giants*, McGraw-Hill, New York, 1997
7   Stross, Randall E., *The Microsoft Way*, Addison-Wesley, New York, 1996
8   Wallace, James, *Overdrive*, John Wiley & Sons, New York, 1997
9   Stross, Randall E., *The Microsoft Way*, Addison-Wesley, New York, 1996
10   Jager, Rama D. and Ortiz, Rafael, *In the Company of Giants*, McGraw-Hill, New York, 1997

CHAPTER 5

1   Jager, Rama D. and Ortiz, Rafael, *In the Company of Giants*, McGraw-Hill, New York, 1997
2   Jager, Rama D. and Ortiz, Rafael, *In the Company of Giants*, McGraw-Hill, New York, 1997

3   Quoted in Napuk, K, 'Live and learn', *Scottish Business Insider*, January 1994
4   Senge, Peter, 'A growing wave of interest and openness', Applewood Internet site, 1997

CHAPTER 6

1   Stross, Randall E., *The Microsoft Way*, Addison-Wesley, New York, 1996
2   Wallace, James and Erickson, Jim, *Hard Drive: Bill Gates and the Making of the Microsoft Empire*, John Wiley, New York, 1992

CHAPTER 7

1   Jager, Rama D. and Ortiz, Rafael, *In the Company of Giants*, McGraw-Hill, New York, 1997
2   Wallace, James and Erickson, Jim, *Hard Drive: Bill Gates and the Making of the Microsoft Empire*, John Wiley & Sons, New York, 1992
3   Kehoe, Louise, 'Engineer of the electronic era', *Financial Times*, January 1, 1995
4   Kehoe, Louise, 'Engineer of the electronic era', *Financial Times*, January 1, 1995
5   Tichy, Noel M., 'The mark of a winner', *Leader to Leader*, Fall 1997
6   Schlender, Brent, 'Bill Gates and Paul Allen talk', *Fortune*, October 2, 1995
7   Kehoe, Louise, 'Engineer of the electronic era', *Financial Times*, January 1, 1995
8   Kehoe, Louise and Dixon, Hugo, 'Fightback at the seat of power', *Financial Times*, June 10, 1996
9   Schwenk, Charles R., 'The case for weaker leadership', *Business Strategy Review*, Autumn 1997

10 Kehoe, Louise, 'Engineer of the electronic era', *Financial Times*, January 1, 1995

CHAPTER 8

1 Kehoe, Louise and Dixon, Hugo, 'The FT Interview', *Financial Times*, June 10, 1996
2 Stross, Randall E., *The Microsoft Way*, Addison-Wesley, New York, 1996
3 Jager, Rama D. and Ortiz, Rafael, *In the Company of Giants*, McGraw-Hill, New York, 1997

CHAPTER 9

1 Cusumano, Michael, 'How Microsoft makes large teams work like small teams', *Sloan Management Review* Vol. 39, No. 1, Fall 1997
2 Peters, Tom, *Liberation Management*, Alfred A. Knopf Inc., 1992
3 Wallace, James, *Overdrive*, John Wiley & Sons, New York, 1997

CHAPTER 10

1 Crainer, Stuart, *The Ultimate Book of Business Quotations*, Capstone, Oxford, 1998
2 Schlender, Brent, 'The Bill and Warren Show', *Fortune*, July 20, 1998
3 Clutterbuck, David, and Goldsmith, Walter, *The Winning Streak Mark II*, Orion, 1997
4 Jager, Rama D. and Ortiz, Rafael, *In the Company of Giants*, McGraw-Hill, New York, 1997

5   Schlender, Brent, 'The Bill and Warren Show', *Fortune*, July 20, 1998

6   Schlender, Brent, 'The Bill and Warren Show', *Fortune*, July 20, 1998

AND FINALLY... KNOW WHEN IT'S TIME TO MOVE ON

1   Bill Gates: A New Era of Technical Leadership at Microsoft. Remarks by Bill Gates, Chairman and Steve Ballmer, CEO, Microsoft Corp. News Conference: A New Era of Technical Leadership at Microsoft Redmond, Washington, June 15, 2006. www.microsoft.com/presspass/exec/billg/speeches/2006/06-15transition.mspx

2   www.computerworld.com/s/article/9056201/Video_Bill_Gates_spoofs_his_retirement

3   Full text: An epic Bill Gates e-mail rant. Microsoft Blog. Seattle PI. Posted by Todd Bishop at June 24, 2008
http://blog.seattlepi.com/microsoft/archives/141821.asp

4   Q&A: Gates talks about letting go, the future and the foundation by Todd Bishop and Tom Paulson. June 23, 2008
www.seattlepi.com/business/368079_gatesqa24ww.html

LAST WORD

1   Stross, Randall E., *The Microsoft Way*, Addison-Wesley, New York, 1996

INDEX

DES DEARLOVE

Des Dearlove's writing career includes more than 10 years as a columnist and commissioning editor for *The Times* (London). His work has appeared in newspapers and magazines worldwide, including the *Financial Times*, the *Industry Standard*, *Business 2.0*, and *Handelsblatt*.

His books are available in more than 20 languages. They include *Business the Richard Branson Way* (now in its 4th edition); and *Generation Entrepreneur* (co-authored with Stuart Crainer), which was a runner-up in the WH Smiths Business Book of the Year award in 2001.

With Stuart Crainer, Des founded Suntop Media and the consulting firm CrainerDearlove, and created the Thinkers 50, the first global ranking of business gurus. Des is an Adjunct Professor at IE Business School, in Madrid.